WILLIAM HURT

WILLIAM HURT

THE MAN THE ACTOR

TOBY GOLDSTEIN

ST. MARTIN'S PRESS • NEW YORK

Special thanks to Dan Yakir for research assistance and, particularly, his incisive theories and insights. Additional thanks to Robin Katz, her friends, and her never-empty file drawers.

WILLIAM HURT:
THE ACTOR AND HIS WORK

For information,
address St. Martin's Press,
175 Fifth Avenue, New York, N.Y. 10010.

Book Design by Peter A. Davis

Library of Congress Cataloging-in-Publication Data

Goldstein, Toby.
William Hurt, the actor and his work.

1. Hurt, William. 2. Actors—United States—
Biography. I. Title.
PN2287.H86G65 1987 791.43'028'0924[B] 87-13980
ISBN 0-312-01113-X

First Edition

10 9 8 7 6 5 4 3 2 1

CONTENTS

INTRODUCTION

Revolution, a formerly hip eating place located at 1 University Place in the heart of Greenwich Village, was a study in coexisting contradictions. At the same time it was a tantalizing and forbidding enclave, a deliberate anachronism that glorified the past while looking toward the future. The restaurant was hung with black-lit neon posters of heroes belonging to another era: Jimi Hendrix, Janis Joplin, Jim Morrison—icons of the sixties counterculture, whose post mortem fame has maintained a longevity approaching their years on earth. These were rooms in which to remember a creative golden age, albeit a time filled with single-minded excesses and obsessiveness that prompted chaos alongside every artistic accomplishment.

Revolution was the place to go for those individuals who needed and wanted to remember when, as well as for the successive generation, born during that turbulent era, who tried to imagine what it all meant, since things are so different now. The legacy of the sixties is one of change, of seeking after the truth, of expressing oneself alone in one's greatest glory, while at the same time commingling with like-minded others. In retrospect, it almost didn't matter that the sixties were doomed, what mattered was that their moments were glorious.

Shortly after Revolution opened on the site of an authentic sixties hangout for artists and domestic revolutionaries, William Hurt and his co-star-companion, Marlee Matlin, were spotted among its patrons. That this couple chose to immerse themselves in an environment dedicated to ferver and torment, with a splash of artistic eternity, made perfect sense. Matlin, at twenty-one, is a feisty, determined child of the sixties—a woman who allows no professional or personal obstacle to interfere with her life's goals. She is the result of a generation who battled to assert their rights and won the opportunity to triumph against seemingly overwhelming odds.

And William Hurt, thirty-six years old at the time, belonged in that room as would few of his contemporaries of the stage and screen. Relentlessly demanding truth, from others as well as himself, Hurt is a constant questioner. He doesn't settle for answers handed to him as gospel, insisting upon forming his own handbook through mental, physical, and spiritual exploration.

On the surface, Hurt resembles the yuppie culture for whom he has become an artistic icon and personal sex symbol. He is six two, lean though well muscled, with a shock of straight blond hair casually swept over his forehead, topping a pair of direct blue eyes in a sculpted face with a broadly cleft chin. Usually dressed in the casual preppie-style uniform suited to his upbringing—button-down shirts, Sta-Prest slacks, slip-ons, wire-rimmed glasses—Hurt nevertheless is far from the stereotypical organization man. He does not conform in any way to the herding instincts of so many of his peers—sixties survivors who now choose to run with the pack on a quest for dollars and the sheltered life in suburbia. In the matter of William Hurt, appearances are very deceiving.

He is, although he finds the term grossly inappropriate to his place in the theatrical community, a movie star. Having been cast in the lead role of his very first motion picture, the

1980 *Altered States,* Hurt was locked into primary parts from then on and has starred in six additional films, with two more in progress. Yet despite the million-dollar fees and significant accolades he has accrued, Hurt insists on maintaining his relationship with the stage, where he has performed every type of theater work from modern relationship dramas to Shakespeare. Throughout his professional career, which in its entirety spans slightly more than a decade, Hurt has opted for those parts which test and ultimately expand his abilities, eschewing far simpler performances that might guarantee huge box-office receipts and the promise of well-paying sequels. Instead of residing in a guarded mansion in one of the film-star havens of California, Hurt lives in an apartment on the Upper West Side of Manhattan, a home within walking distance of Lincoln Center and only a short cab ride from Broadway.

His success is perhaps partially explained by the fact that William Hurt appears to be a man for all eras. To those who cherish fond memories of the turbulent sixties, Hurt casts a long shadow as the valued individual, defying a society he deems stultifying in order to fulfill his own inner directive. In none of his roles has William Hurt blindly followed orders. Rather, he ferrets out unstoppable truths, and if those discoveries threaten the orderly pattern of his character's existence, so much the better. He is seen as reckless, if not in an overtly political way then in his private philosophy. In each of his roles, Hurt has aimed to make an essential discovery about life, with as much zeal for each part as the tempestuous street missionary brings to his calling. Indeed, some have ventured the opinion that William Hurt sees himself in religious imagery, his devotion to establishing a pure art apart from society's precepts finding a parallel in the messiahs' reveling in spiritual gratification far distant from earthly measures of contentment and satisfaction.

"I've never entered into a situation where I felt I had the answers," Hurt has said. "I would botch it if I did, because it would become an exercise in neurosis. You have to be stable enough to pose the questions. . . . Acting is not psychoanalysis, not acting out, nor a personal catharsis for me—in any sense, primal or transient. It's a craft through which I ask a question, a number of questions, that entertain and interest me."

If Hurt's constant questioning for the purpose of his characters' self-discovery and his own enlightenment establishes his roots in the sixties, then the tenderness, deep feelings, and respect so many of his characters display toward their women make the actor acceptable as a "new man," that elusive masculine entity first alluded to during the seventies. While painfully establishing their own identities, with every step forward a battle, women fed up with their objectification yearned for a man who would treat them with respect, who would encourage their own development and pay as much attention to the relationship as the women themselves were expected to.

In the majority of his roles, William Hurt has played the kind of man who is motivated—whether internally or because of a crisis—to communicate with his romantic counterpart. This was shown most dramatically in Hurt's 1986 film, *Children of a Lesser God,* in which he had to literally learn a new language—the sign language of the deaf—to meet the woman he loves on her terms. But even when not depicted so obviously, Hurt's characters respond to powerful women, women established in their own careers, and value those strengths in the relationship. Many so-called new men fell out of favor because they were eventually perceived to be wimps. However, Hurt's inner fire and his own self-confidence has kept him at a safe distance from that fate.

And in the decade now winding down, the qualities an audience admires have changed again, but once more, William Hurt has satisfied the needs of his viewers. His Waspish good looks find favor with the corporate-suited legions, who can relate to his rangy frame. Obviously, Hurt keeps himself in good shape. And while in his movies he does not always play a professional, Hurt is always shown to be a man of intelligence and perceptiveness. He usually figures out the answers first, and even in the case of *Body Heat,* where his Ned Racine loses to Kathleen Turner's Matty Walker, the epitome of the conniving woman, Hurt admires the game when it's played against a worthy adversary.

Shortly after *Altered States* premiered in 1980, William Hurt was described as "the thinking woman's pinup," a characterization that has grown more apt with each successive role. Hurt satisfies the lust of body and mind for an ever-expanding circle of filmgoers, yet he has never resorted to the quick kill of an easy, sexual, box-office sell to increase his viewership. "They are antithetical to the idea of theater," he labeled the Rambos and Dirty Harrys of cinema. "Our job as actors is to perceive our humanity. That's our work, not the creation of pathological heroes." Instead, in the film that won him an Academy Award, *Kiss of the Spider Woman,* Hurt played an undisguised homosexual. Typically, he showed no apprehension or hesitancy about how playing the role of a societal outcast might affect the career of an up-and-coming, confirmed heterosexual actor.

"If you think about that, you're thinking wrong," he declared. "If I quantify my work, I'm cutting off. I'm throttling myself. I'm not growing. I've lost the purpose of my work, which is to explore and witness, and sing and . . . discover.

"Don't condescend," he said, as much to himself as to his interviewer, "because condescension is such a terrible insult. For instance, if I hear a director say to me, 'Well, how did you make the audience feel this?' I don't make anyone feel anything. I don't want anybody telling me what to think or feel and I don't want to tell anyone else what to think or feel. To me there's a lot more joy and depth in this little existence than that. And me manipulating someone else . . . I don't like being manipulated and I don't like manipulating. So what I do is to try and use my form to observe things and explore things, for as much as possible for its own sake. And I think we are all using that form for that. Our ticket is our curiosity. That's what gets you in the door, and that's the way it ought to be, and that's the way it should stay."

Though he is often impenetrable when wrestling with the issues of his craft, William Hurt has spent his life affirming the value of being human, a theme that he brings out with every performance. He portrays characters with openness and compassion, with the willingness to be scalded that marks the great romantics of art. Whatever he risks, he gets more back, thanks to the effort. William Hurt revels in the glory of love, and there is no more fulfilling, long-lasting reward for a thinking, caring, adventurous human being.

"I am personally obsessed," he admitted some time ago. "I had a dream once, and the dream said, 'Truth and beauty.' But how do you say that to someone without them saying, 'We are all searching for truth and beauty?'"

1

ISSUES WITHOUT ANSWERS

A CHILDHOOD OF CHANGE

William Hurt was born into a world full of secrets: the secrets of power, that most tantalizing aphrodesiac, which swirls around the Washington, D.C. corridors that were his father's home base. The senior Hurt was a director of trust territories for the U.S. State Department, a job entailing constant movement for himself, his wife, and their three children. Although William first saw the light of day in the nation's capital, on March 20, 1950, it wasn't long before the family moved to the South Pacific. It was an idyllic existence for the little boy and his two brothers, one older and one younger, and figures prominently in Hurt's earliest memories.

"Until I was six, I was living in this paradise in the South Pacific. My brothers and I were *bad* little boys on Guam. We used to sit in mud puddles during typhoons. We used to explore the Quonset huts that were out in the boondocks, left by the troops from World War Two. Sometimes we'd get a little ambitious and we'd burn the huts down. Then all the fathers would have to run out of their offices and put out the fires and chase these half-naked kids through the jungle."

What a delicious sense of freedom for a young, developing mind and body. He and his playmates were not confined by the cautionary rules and regulations that temper urban living and restrain its children. The Hurts could dress in the bare minimum demanded by tropical climates and come to know nature with a sense of intimacy. No walls of concrete interfered with the young Hurt's awareness of the elements. And though life in the South Pacific during the fifties was not glittering, Hurt's family enjoyed the perks of an officer's existence. Their quarters were the best; they wanted for nothing. Materially and spiritually, they were unbounded.

"Living in the South Pacific I got used to the kind of freedom and abandon that few people will ever really know," he mused. "An atmosphere of tropical paradise. Swimming, surfing, walking around half-naked with nobody caring. Coming back into New York from the airport, I thought the buildings would fall on me. I had never seen one higher than seven stories."

When Hurt was just six years old his parents divorced. An epidemic of contemporary times, such an event was not as common during the mid-fifties. Children of divorce could not automatically find a half-dozen other neighborhood kids who had experienced the same traumatic dissolution. More often than not, a child of divorce was alone except for his siblings, having to deal with arguments, tears, and lengthy separations as if such a tragedy had never occurred to any other innocent kid in the whole world.

Although Hurt, having two brothers, was not forced to face the end of his secure family unit completely bereft of companionship, the divorce brought with it a different kind of disruption. Sheared away from the carefree attitudes of the tropical islands, Hurt began the next phase of his life on a very different island—Manhattan. It was, naturally, a terrifying transition. The boy who had played wildly in torrential rainstorms without fear became a boy who hid under his mother's skirts at the arrivals terminal, overwhelmed by the crowds, noise, and sheer massiveness of his new homeland.

The family settled into a modest four-room apartment on the Upper West Side, a neighborhood at that time light-years away from the haven of wealth it has since become. The towering apartment buildings, with their polished brass railings, canopies, and doormen, dominated Central Park West, but once you turned the corner onto a side street, the glamour was gone. Undifferentiated brick apartment buildings rubbed shoulders with run-down brownstones, single-room-occupancy hotels, and dangerous-looking tenements. Gangs prowled the neighborhood, each defending its turf with fists, knives, and chains. William Hurt's four years on the West Side were spent at a time when street violence was pervasive enough to mark the territory as the location for the 1957 hit Broadway play, *West Side Story*. Even a schoolchild had to measure his paces very carefully and develop an awareness that trouble might be waiting just behind his shoulder. What helped him through was the love of his family. "When my mother and my brothers and I were living together, no matter how much we fought each other, we had the notion that if anybody turned against any one of us, together we couldn't be beaten."

Only the summer vacations offered William respite from the pressures of New York street life. Each year when school ended, Hurt fled the broiling pavement for a reunion with his father, which frequently meant a trip to some new, exotic locale. While most kids consider themselves fortunate to have visited Disneyland, Hurt spent time in the Sudan, Somaliland, Pakistan, and Spain before he turned eighteen.

William Hurt got to know about the world and its possibilities, but still a child, he was able to absorb only a percentage of its powerful influences. Yet he heard strange languages, saw bizarre styles of clothing, witnessed unusual customs, and knew that to the people of the world, their way of living was as normal as his blue jeans, skinned knees, and American slang was to him. What was different came to be respected and proved a continual source of fascination. Inside the boy a man was developing who would find intense appeal in uncovering the widest range of human behavior: how people lived and loved around the world was a source of wonder—and inspiration.

However, all of Hurt's global consciousness did not prepare him for the next twist of fate which befell his family. When he was ten and had more or less grown used to being just another Manhattan kid, his mother remarried. The person she had fallen in love with was Henry Luce III, the man whose father had founded *Time* magazine. So far, Hurt had adapted to the wild tropics and the equally wild Manhattan byways. But another abrupt switch in life-styles, this one an upward leap to the rarefied corridors of extreme wealth and power, was more than a sensitive youth could easily handle.

Luce brought his wife and stepchildren to surroundings that suited their station in life, a twenty-two-room duplex quite removed from the dark corners of the West Side. At the time, the publishing magnate was having a splendid skyscraper built along Sixth Avenue to house his burgeoning print empire. While the Time & Life Building was being constructed, business was conducted from the thirty-fourth floor of Rockefeller Center, right across the street. Once, years later, entering the magnificent art deco complex in midtown Manhattan, Hurt exclaimed, "I used to live here!" and set about examining the murals as if with a child's eyes.

It was all very grand and stocked with luxuries few could imagine, even in their dreams. But to William, upward mobility mattered less than the fact that he was again being removed from something familiar into a world of unknown perils. Life at the top took its toll, and he developed a phobia of being in New York at all. The solution, it was decided for him, was to send the child away to boarding school. The boy who had painfully learned to look after himself on the streets was now faced with surviving in the upper-class world of Middlesex Prep School in Massachusetts, away from everything that was familiar to him.

"I went from a pretty rough section of town to the Ivy League," he recalled. "All of a sudden I found myself in Bass Weejuns, white socks, herringbone jackets, ties, study halls, dormitories, with the upper crust, with people who didn't know anything of what I had been through and couldn't share it. I was so alienated from the world I found myself in that I created a very hard situation for myself."

Add to that the fact that as a youth, Hurt was short and fat; the result was a guaranteed setup for his becoming a victim. Being put-upon by other, comelier children merely escalated the anger and self-destructiveness burning in the boy because he was so insecure. As Hurt remembered his years at Middlesex, he recalled the ways in which he would sabotage himself, only digging himself deeper into a trough of despair.

"You know, in school, when something went wrong and the teacher said, 'If whoever did this doesn't come up, the whole class will be punished,' I'd raise my hand even though I hadn't done it. At that point I started separating myself from other people. I started telling convincing tall stories and I'd pick fights. I'd pick fights with these big guys that I invariably lost because I was short, fat, and uncoordinated.

"I was also lousy at athletics. I came back to school early for football tryouts, hoping to be on the varsity team, and ended up on the smallest team. And even then, if there were seven for the six-man team, I didn't play. It was a hell of a time—the kill ethic—and I wrecked my back."

Aware of William's festering emotions, one of his teachers thought he might enjoy releasing some of his anger in a more controlled, positive manner—on the stage. Having first taken part in a fourth grade class pageant called *The Stars and Stripes,* in which he played George Washington, Hurt followed the instructor's advice and realized that he enjoyed stagecraft, as well as appreciating the release it gave him. Although acknowledging himself as "naturally an actor," Hurt admitted he had a stroke of luck in that a theater teacher was the one to have inspired him. His debut performance at Middlesex was in the role of Billy in Dylan Thomas's *Under Milk Wood*—played before an audience of forty. While a rewarding diversion from the problems of adolescence, acting did not immediately implant itself in Hurt's consciousness as the only career for him. He continued to take part in school productions but did not foresee carrying the extracurricular activity any further.

Instead, Hurt completed his preparatory education, which became a lot easier to bear after he grew six inches in thirteen months, reaching a height of over six feet, and lost the extra pounds of baby fat. He continued to travel the world in the summertime, visiting his father and perfecting skills that diverged greatly from the well-ordered environment at school. A dedicated fisherman today, William had learned to hunt as a consequence of having lived where he had but shelved hunting forever during his teens.

He explained, "The day I stopped even dreaming about hunting was in Somaliland, when a friend of my father's took me out with him. He took my father's old .303 Lee-Enfield, a classic military gun that Kipling wrote about. It was very powerful, very accurate—a really great gun. Unfortunately, it kills things.

"My father had a scope mounted on it, and this guy laid it on the hood of a Land-Rover. There was a gazelle that, it turned out later, was five-sixths of a mile away. And he nailed it. And I decided that I was never going to hunt that way in my life. It was too distant, too abstract." The fundamental experiences of life, whether painful or blessedly joyous, had to be palpable for Hurt. Whether in his own life or in his roles, little occurs at great remove from his core.

Graduating from prep school at eighteen, Hurt was surrounded within and without by the passions of the time. Outside his sheltered enclave of morals and manners, students were fighting with police in the streets. Young men of lesser means were being shipped off in daily planeloads to a Southeast Asia far different than the one Hurt took for granted. Vietnam extracted its merciless quota of mortal wounds and crippling injuries. On those fields, the sun shone upon tormented, screaming casualties, not the laughter of small, carefree boys. Back at home, what was termed the counterculture turned to the appeal of hallucinogens to escape grappling with the blood and fury that was late sixties America. And there was William

Hurt—wealthy, young, healthy, but without answers to tell him where the meaning of his life lay.

Hoping to find a message that would explain and soothe the turbulence around him, Hurt enrolled in Tufts University as a theology major. "I wanted to be saved," he admitted, "and I also wanted to earn the love of my stepfather, who was a very important man in my life. I ran into serious problems when my mother remarried, but that man has since become the greatest teacher I have ever known. He improved my life immensely." After graduating, Hurt had every intention of entering the church. To prepare him for such an intellectually and spiritually demanding vocation, he looked to his religion classes as a much needed forum in which to grapple with the eternal human question: *Why?*

"I tried to use religious philosophy to become better informed, to be able to make a better choice. I love the ritual of religion, which is like the ritual of theater. It is about imagination, people gathering together, telling each other what to believe." Yet, by the end of his second year, Hurt's world view had again changed substantially, and he switched his major to drama.

He explained, "I was choosing one of two egotistical things to do, to be an actor or a minister. But maybe that's more egotistical—to stand up and say, 'God's my best friend, and if you want to get to know him you've got to get to know me!' I didn't think I was equipped to say that. So if I wanted to do something selfish, something that I wanted to do, it had to be acting."

As a drama student, Hurt found personal fulfillment as well as dedication to the art. He met and married a young actress in the spring of his junior year. That fall, Hurt and his wife, Mary Beth, moved to London, where he completed his senior year of college, graduating with honors. Hurt benefited greatly from the British concentration on acting technique, since his early performances had emotional weight at their center but needed refining. Yet when choosing where to pursue his postgraduate training, Hurt felt that America would serve him best. "I decided on America because I preferred the passion that seeks the form rather than the form that seeks the passion," he declared.

In New York for a friend's funeral, Hurt impetuously decided to audition for several acting schools, including the performer's acme, the Juilliard School. NYU and Yale declined his request for an audition, but Juilliard granted him one, although on very short notice. "They said be there at ten A.M. with forty bucks and two pieces, one comic and one tragic, one modern and one classic." He had already been learning the John Osborne play *Look Back in Anger* and put three short segments together for a monologue. Then Hurt and his stepbrother Kit combed Kit's apartment for a classical work, until they found a copy of Shakespeare's *King Lear.* Kit helped him memorize one of Lear's soliloquies, which they finished six hours before the audition.

Hurt and his wife were back in England when they learned that he had been accepted by the school. They returned to New York and settled, as befitted their near-starving-artist status, in a fourth-floor walk-up apartment on the Lower East Side. Posthippie and pregentrification, the East Village of the early seventies was a seamy stew of poverty-stricken welfare families, aging, fearful old Ukranian immigrants, some leftover flower people, and a raft of junkies—the casualties of a long-ago Summer of Love. Some of the wretched refuse lived next door to the Hurts in a fleabag hotel and used to throw bottles against the couple's windows.

While William studied and established friendships with fellow students Robin Williams, Christopher Reeve, and Kevin Kline, Mary Beth worked as a seamstress to help make ends meet. During the three years that Hurt spent at Juilliard, his marriage began to deteriorate. Eventually, the couple divorced, though Hurt did reveal to *Rolling Stone* reporter Carol Caldwell in 1981, "She was the truest love I've ever had, Mary Beth. A true foundation of love and trust. You wonder why you ever contested marriage as a backward notion of society. It's not. It never ends, whether you divorce or not."

At the same time that his personal life was being stressed, Hurt began to recognize his increasing difficulties with the program at Juilliard. "I learned a tremendous amount," he acknowledged, "but I always was at odds with the institution and wanted to get away." The anger that never seems far from Hurt's frustration threshold led him into arguments with his teachers. To make everything even worse, his mother passed away, leaving a profound void.

"My mother was a powerful influence in my life," he later said. "She was a remarkable businesswoman, remarkable artistically and emotionally. Because I was the middle son I was regarded as the ameliorator. I miss her. She would have enjoyed what happened to me."

At odds with the way his education was at a stalemate, confused by his marital problems, distraught over his personal loss, Hurt felt that he had to get away from New York or he would burst. With just a short while to go before graduation, Hurt left Juilliard and bought himself a four-cylinder Honda. In the time-honored tradition of the searching, tormented soul, Hurt hit the road and again sought solace from places he'd never seen before. This time, Hurt explored America, as he traveled from the East Coast to the West Coast, searching in the cities and towns he passed through for some clue as to how he should live his life. Hurt rode all the way to San Francisco, then turned north, passing through the lush, still largely unspoiled Pacific Northwest.

Unexpectedly, the insight he longed for came to him in the town of Ashland, Oregon. A Shakespeare festival was in progress, and Hurt accepted the offer to join its company. Uncaring of the fact that he was dropping out of Juilliard only one month before his studies would have officially been ended, William Hurt found his direction as he took on the role of Edmund in Eugene O'Neill's *Long Day's Journey Into Night.*

He said, "I had worked for years in complete darkness, complete doubt, complete confusion. And then one day I walked out onstage and realized I had some craft. It was just *there,* and it felt so good."

For the first time, Hurt discovered something in himself that didn't yield to doubt and wasn't subject to stresses placed upon him by others, or for that matter, by his own self-destructive tendencies. He had found purpose in being on a stage, and felt confident that he would be its master. "I have no compunction about saying I was the best Edmund there ever was," he boldly stated.

2

AN ACTOR IS MADE

There are actors, and there are stars, and there are cities that cultivate each. The differences can be seen in the aspirations of newcomers, the fresh-faced optimists who toil at waiter's jobs or serve as parking lot attendants to the rich and famous. Los Angeles is the preferred locale of these would-be film giants and television celebrities—the people who form the stock-in-trade of fan clubs and gossip columns. The lucky few who strike it big learn to live with flashbulbs constantly exploding in their faces and deal with the paranoia of instant celebrity by spending large chunks of their megabuck salaries on barricaded palaces. The actors of Hollywood realize that they have been paid a large entrance fee to enter the public's domain, and for most of them, the reward justifies the resulting lack of privacy.

In New York, however, the environment is as different from L.A.'s expansiveness as Manhattan's winter slush is from a day of California sunshine. With, until very recently, no indigenous film or prime-time television industry basing itself on the East Coast, actors were left with several options, none of them mania inducing. A fortunate handful can earn relatively steady money as cast members of daytime soap operas, though for many years that medium was unfairly deprecated as shallow and undemanding. In other words, it may have been the only way for an actor to pay the bills on time, but as far as critics and fellow thespians were concerned, it wasn't art. Still, Jill Clayburgh, Christopher Reeve and Kevin Bacon, among many, many others, took on roles in soaps early in their careers.

Most of the New York acting community opted for the stage, where the training was rigorous, the hours long, and the pay little more than an unemployment check. Except for the few principals of a Broadway show, actors rarely earned enough money to rent themselves more than a cold-water walk-up flat in a seedy Manhattan neighborhood—that is, a decade or so ago, when undesirable real estate actually existed in New York.

They acted, and in large measure, still do, without expectations of a sudden catapult into big money or fame. Day after day, they cluster into classes, refining their speech, honing their technique, aiming for a higher level than the one they hit the day before. They do it for a love of the craft, the chance to step on a stage in a role that carries some meaning, to move an audience that may number in the hundreds, or in the dozens, to describe a world not bound by the conventions of commerce, including commercial art. They act because, in many cases, they cannot imagine spending their lives doing anything else.

"The perfection of the theater is that it's over the second it's done," William Hurt once said. "It's such a beautiful and immediate image of what acting is all about. I am a disciplined and well-trained actor. I can wrap ten meanings around one word in two seconds. That's not boasting, it's just flagrant, baroque, useless talent. Why do I have to show off how technically proficient I am? I have a passionate vision, but it's there to express and not manipulate. That's why I call myself an actor."

Hurt's transcendant experience in Oregon proved that the demands of acting would forever stake a claim on his soul. He also performed in *King Lear* in Ashland, and then wended his way back east. En route, at the Meadowbrook Theatre in Detroit, he accepted the demanding role of Tanner in George Bernard Shaw's *Man and Superman,* mastering the lengthy part in only four days. Rapturous on the subject of Shaw, Hurt would find the Irish chronicler of human strengths and foibles a safe haven, while he wrestled with mastery over other, less personally accessible works.

"Your basic approach to any character is the same, whether it's Restoration, Jacobean, Elizabethan, modern; no matter what the character might be, whether he's got six arms and five legs, you know, and one gigantic pimple on the end of his nose. Your approach basically is the same. You will end up looking for one thing—the theme of the play or the movie—and if you have chosen well, you probably shouldn't come to a satisfactory idea about it in your lifetime. . . ." Hurt trailed off, realizing that he was reinforcing his own self-doubts.

"But Shaw is my favorite," the actor proclaimed. "I've done nearly all of his. It took me a long time to get my mind around Shakespeare. I couldn't do it. I couldn't understand. I knew he was there, I knew he was great. I just couldn't find him, you know, but I could always find Shaw. And to me, if you cut just one word out of Shaw you're doing him a great disservice because he knew what he was doing. And anyone who thinks he's wordy is full of shit." So there. As Hurt developed his art and began to win both critical accolades and the praise of audiences, such devotion to words would make perfect sense. The actor himself has a love of words that frequently manifests itself in lengthy philosophical treatises or allegorical ramblings, often before a group that finds keeping up with him a challenge. On more than one occasion, interviewers have been left at the starting gate, bewildered, as Hurt launched into one of his monologues.

At one point, the actor acknowledged his tendency to, as he put it, "get all spaced," but defended the validity of his own visions, even if they weren't readily comprehensible.

"I had fantasies about living in the wrong time or wishing that I were, I don't know, Louis XIV. . . . But this is not what's happening. You try to build your imagination and deal with that, while staying in the here and now. Some people—myself included—have trouble doing that. You have to live who you are. I'm not inventive enough to build my own missile and go live somewhere else, on another planet.

"Sometimes I'll get all spaced—and it's a place that I know well—but a lot of people don't understand it at all. They come up to me and say, 'What's wrong?' And I say, 'I'm here. Nothing's wrong. I'm myself.' But they feel rebuffed and insulted, and it's not that at all. The greatest compliment I can pay anybody is by being with them and by allowing myself to feel what I feel in their company. I could, after all, walk out of there."

To fulfill his greatest potential, William Hurt needed to find a group of actors who would value his eccentricities as well as his genius. "I need feedback from other actors, an ensemble situation," he stated. "If I have any ambition of being an artist—and I do, even if it means I'm going through another adolescence—this is something I refuse to give up." Upon returning to New York in 1976, Hurt discovered a company of actors that would nurture and inspire him—a group with whom he could be himself and allow his repertoire to expand past any self-imposed limitations.

Hurt had already made his television debut by the time he came home to stay. In fact, he appeared in programs that catered to two very different segments of the viewing audience: a PBS dramatic series called "The Best of Families," and in a two-part episode of "Kojak," the latter surviving as one of his lesser known credits. (Bearded, all but unrecognizable in a bulky jumpsuit, Hurt was onscreen for about thirty seconds per episode, in the role of a law student involved in one of the bald detective's numerous homicide investigations. Sadly, his character enjoyed only about a dozen lines of dialogue before he, too, became another bullet-riddled body for Theo Kojak to fret over.) Hurt also performed in *Henry V* at the New York Shakespeare Festival during that early era.

Nineteen seventy-six marked the beginning of a productive and still ongoing relationship between William Hurt and the Circle Repertory Company, probably New York's most prestigious independent theater group. Its members, all dedicated professionals, adhere to no boundaries in selecting their repertoire, which ranges from the most esteemed classics to highly experimental modern works. Playwright Corinne Jacker, author of "The Best of Families," asked

Hurt to read for her new play, *My Life*, as a result of his performance on the public television broadcast. He landed the part of Eddie Howe, described as "a young physicist swimming in memories," and made an immediate impact on the company's founder and artistic director, Marshall Mason, when rehearsals of the production began the following year.

"There was an instantaneous rapport from the first rehearsal," Mason told an interviewer from *New York* magazine, "and few moments of doubt since then." To *Time* magazine, Mason lauded the actor's "generosity and anger, his sensitivity and scathing sense of humor—all this and lots of sexual heat." For his part, Hurt sensed an aura of acceptance awaiting him at Circle Rep. "It was," he said, "like walking into my own home. All the things I had been thinking about for so long were in focus there. Marshall's work was like breathing for me." The Circle Rep has been home to William Hurt since that time, providing him with most of his critically lauded stage roles, and he still considers himself a member of the troupe.

Hurt's performance in *My Life* resulted in immediate recognition of the young actor's uncaged abilities. He won Off Broadway's highest honor, an Obie, as well as the Theatre World Award for distinguished stage debut. Hurt has never been a man to sit around and plan his future on the basis of his reviews, but by the end of his first year with the repertory company, the word was out that William Hurt was an up-and-comer. Beneath the cool blond exterior, he performed with emotions afire. Cynthia Heimel, writing in the *Soho Weekly News,* said of his performance as the tormented priest, Father Rivard, in *The Runner Stumbles*, another Circle

Rep production, "It was interesting to watch him onstage. The other members of the cast were emoting their asses off, and very well, too—Hurt seemed like a guy in his living room to whom some mighty strange things were happening. You can't help but pay attention."

And Hurt drew such attention even when surrounded by his peers, some of whom were equally handsome and compelling. For instance, Christopher Reeve played the role of Hurt's father in *My Life*.

Hurt followed up these early triumphs with new roles that challenged him, trying always to explore new facets of the human condition, never opting for parts that were simply walk-throughs. Within the next few years, he originated the role of Ken Talley, the paraplegic homosexual Vietnam veteran in Lanford Wilson's *Fifth of July;* played the lead role of the impotent playwright in Albert Innaurato's *Ulysses in Traction*—a part created especially for him; and appeared in Franz Wedekind's *Lulu* and in the Circle Rep's own staging of *Hamlet.* Critic Clive Barnes judged the latter performance, "a marker stone in the career of a great actor."

Each performance was a fresh opportunity for the actor, and he relished the start-up, enjoying its possibilities. Even though the focus was turning with greater frequency upon him as a lead, he commented, "With the Circle, which is an ensemble theater, I don't feel anxious about getting attention. I feel respected. If I'm not getting attention it doesn't mean that I'm not being listened to.

"Slowly, a new play tells me what to do, or failing that, I try to listen to myself and spell out the options. If you are really far away from the play there are tools [you can use], but you first must sift through your first impressions and try to find for yourself the first step, whether it's the theme, or the action, or your relationship to the other people. Everybody in the play wants the same thing, but the way they get it is at odds. You have to feel for what the play wants. A spine takes on flesh and then is a body."

The Circle helped Hurt set aside his insecurities and doubts in favor of some good old-fashioned, dedicated sweat. "I need Circle to breathe," he said, "it's the best form of energy that I can get. I've never worked at a place where more of what I am is where they are going."

By 1978, Hurt's theatrical triumphs, and the deep-seated sensuality critics loved pointing out, had not escaped the notice of Hollywood. Hurt admitted he wasn't a fan of the place. "I promised myself I wouldn't go to L.A. without a job and a return ticket in my hand." He worried about protecting his privacy in the land of floodlights, and turned down several feature film offers. One that he desired, but which got away, was *Oliver's Story*. Hurt was not impressed with the original screenplay, but changed his mind after director John Korty rewrote it. Coveting the part, Hurt had one group of people on his side, but lost out when superstar Ryan O'Neal announced that he was willing to do it. Paramount, typically, opted to use a known box office attraction (who had, after all, starred in Oliver's original tale, *Love Story*) over a newcomer, however attractive, and Hurt, momentarily derailed, returned to the type of productions he knew best. He was willing to live on the two hundred dollars a week Circle Rep was able to pay its company—enough to pay a cheap rent, even if it didn't allow for any luxuries.

When actress Sally Kellerman got her first look at William Hurt, her comment was straight from the, ahem, loins: "Now that's what I call a gorgeous hunk of man." Hurt was teamed with Kellerman and another skyrocketing film luminary, Sissy Spacek, for his second appearance on public television, *Verna: U.S.O. Girl.* Set in World War II Europe and focusing on the exploits of a touring U.S.O. entertainment troup, the play brought Hurt into proximity with a group of actors who managed to retain their sense of quality despite being well-established names. It also generated the actor's first fan letters, which he admitted took some getting used to. When the New York *Post*'s "People" page bannered VERNA MAN SHOWS POTENTIAL and said that he was the new Robert Redford, Hurt's acting buddies responded in the only thing they could to such a serious performer: they started calling him Billy Bob.

Hurt found working with film stars on *Verna* an unexpected pleasure. He hadn't previously accepted the possibility of keeping your own and your audience's respect if you were the kind of player that people besieged for autographs. But Spacek and Kellerman did manage to do just that, and their lack of affectation was something else he found noteworthy. "My experience with Sissy Spacek and Sally Kellerman was amazing, finding out firsthand that they really are incredibly talented people. Sissy and I came together like a thunderclap. I've never hit it off on a professional basis that quickly or that powerfully with anybody. I found out that I could relax and do what I do and it would have to be all right."

He was not yet thirty, and William Hurt found himself viewed by his peers, his audiences, and the critics as a leading man, when in fact he still saw himself as part of an ensemble. He didn't feel completely at ease being singled out for attention but recognized that, even if he played character parts, his career was being mapped out in a direction that very soon would only include major landmarks. "I'm a character man in a leading man's body," he told Judy Klemesrud of *The New York Times*. "I love character roles. I'm trained for them. I have much more fun playing them." But once established as a star, Hurt was faced with the challenge of making his leading roles into authentic characters. It was a task he rose to with gusto and would accomplish admirably.

During the next few years, Hurt became unexpectedly involved with the world of films, as the elusive scripts he hoped one day to receive—with parts that were not insulting to his intelligence—began to pour in. Success compounded success, and the actor began to attract the attention of the entertainment community at large. Still, he identified himself as a stage actor first and foremost, and he was not easily pulled away from the bond he felt with a live audience. Though expressed in a rather bizarre context, which would pain him everytime a journalist brought it up, Hurt once described his purpose onstage as an actor in terms of an out-of-body experience.

"I was acting once," he said, "and I went and sat in the back row and watched myself acting. I don't know how to compartmentalize it for you. I think most people have it, frankly. Let's say you're walking out of your hotel and some eight-foot-tall guy weighing five hundred pounds comes up to you and says, 'Give me every penny you've got, or I'll knock the shit out of you.' Well, you are probably going to give him what he wants, but at the same time it might seem funny. I mean, your awareness is heightened. But we get complacent, we don't notice things like this.

"Maybe adrenaline causes us to see things more clearly. There are differentiating circumstances. But the truth does not essentially change. The truth of existence and consciousness does not change. Because that may have something to do with the meaning of consciousness. I mean, what is a thought? It's an interesting question. You see, I think thoughts have lives. Not exactly lives separate from ourselves. But there's a strong feeling of duality, and of oneness, too. It's the same thing. I see a circle and a center and I know the circle is the center, and the center is the circle. And yet they're not the same."

Theories that betrayed Hurt's extensive grounding in religion and philosophy often left his questioners in the dust, wondering whether the intense young actor was really speaking the same language, or even occupied the same planet. However, underneath the admittedly confusing rambles was a world view that attempted to link human beings of different backgrounds together rather than separate them. For Hurt, acting was not an ivory tower profession that advocated aloofness; it was a means of understanding how alike we fundamentally are to one another.

He concluded, "What was being shown to me was that my body was in no way ultimately more important than the guy sitting in the back row of the third tier. His heart was taking as many risks beating every second as mine was. And that's what it's all about. It's not about me more than it is about you. It's about you because it's about me. So I'll face myself and if we can find that interesting, then great. If we can't, then I'll look for something else."

By the time that Hurt returned to the Circle Rep's tiny Off Broadway theater in the lead of *Childe Byron* in 1981, his first encounters with Hollywood were already adhering to his coattails. Some observers were surprised that an instant film star—which, like it or not, was what Hurt had become—would even desire to return to the more modest rewards of the stage. Others recognized the actor's loyalty to the troupe that had nurtured him and helped him develop such praiseworthy talents.

Childe Byron, by Romulus Linney, had premiered in 1977 at the Virginia Museum Theater in Richmond. Originally, the script had been optioned for a Broadway play, with Hurt's contemporary, Christopher Walken, set to appear in the leading role. When those plans fell through, Linney sent the script to Marshall Mason, who staged it for his company. The play opened at the Circle Repertory Theatre on February 26, 1981. Immediately, critics made haste to distance the play, which they disliked, from the leading actors, upon whom they lavished kind words. "I feel a little dizzy," the playwright admitted as *Childe Byron* was about to open. At the time, Linney had three productions simultaneously being readied for New York debuts. "With three new works, a lot of things can go wrong."

The play's theme centers upon the relationship between the passionate, often eccentric romantic poet, Lord Byron, and his daughter, Ada. Byron's ghost returns from the dead to visit Ada on the last day of her life—a scenario that allows for a recap of the poet's own life and times. According to local press reactions, the story turned out to be clumsy and abrupt, largely cutting off any valid emotional audience response.

Said *New York Times* critic Frank Rich, "Mr. Linney may scatter his evening with readings from Byron's works and some of the poet's wittier lines, but his attempt at biographical theater recalls television's 'This Is Your Life.'" *Village Voice* reviewer Jan Hoffman was disturbed by the play's many historical inaccuracies, but even more outraged by the author's early promise that the story would be told from the perspective of Ada, and his subsequent focusing upon Byron to the exclusion of his daughter. She wrote, "Linney's difficulties arose when he couldn't decide whether to hand the play over to Ada or Byron. . . . This project was to be hers, spun from her fever . . . But when it's finally her turn, after some two lopsided hours of Byron, her story is given a hasty wrap-up, as if Linney's rushing to give us the general idea before she kicks the bucket. . . . *Childe Byron* muddles both stories, and the child is not mother to the man."

Still, the reviewers refused to blame the actors for the sins of the playwright and were generous with their observations of the piece's costars. Lindsay Crouse, who had appeared as Ophelia opposite William Hurt's Hamlet in the Circle Rep's previous season, was dubbed by the *Times* "a gifted actress who keeps getting better and better. These two actors are exciting to watch, no matter what they do, but let's hope that next year they'll reunite once again in a real play."

And both critics were encouraging with their comments about Hurt. He was seen as being able to rise above the uneven material he had been given to work with. When the actor's innate powers of persuasion took over from the script, he left the watchers breathless, eager to discover what he might do next. William Hurt had been unleashed upon the film world, a much wider arena than the theater, but at least in the eyes of many local observers, it had not diminished him one bit. The *Times:* "Maybe William Hurt has now been discovered by Hollywood, but he hasn't lost any of that crazy intensity that makes him a joy to watch in the theater. What makes this talented actor so special—and inevitably, a star—is his ability to create his own reality on stage." The *Voice:* "Go to bask in the Byronic acting. [Hurt] makes large, extraordinary gestures, which he then clips off, like a neat phrase from *Don Juan.* The legs sprawl, the head's thrown back—throat curving, chest arched. His intelligence checks everything right before he converges on grandstanding. The play's flaws tiptoe quietly offstage, and we watch a performance.

"William Hurt really is up to the fifteen minutes of fame the press has conferred upon him this week."

He was only thirty years old, already a star of stage and, now, of the small screen. William Hurt's catapulting to national renown from local hero was seen as marvelous by many—those who understood that an intelligent and emotive talent would not stay confined for very long. His Obie after only two years as a professional actor was proof that Hurt's peers respected his abilities. His loyalty to the Circle Rep, even after Hollywood had beckoned with large sums of cash, was proof that Hurt took his acting seriously and would not be tempted into playing lesser roles as a tradeoff for superstardom. Still, in the eyes of some observers, William Hurt had come a little too far, a little too fast.

Perhaps he hadn't suffered enough, spent a sufficient number of tortured years waiting tables, or known the pangs of rude rejection at actors' cattle calls. For one critic, *The Village Voice*'s Gordon Rogoff, Hurt was simply too young to feel at ease with the kind of accolades he had begun to receive. "In America," wrote Rogoff, "the real danger is to have greatness thrust prematurely upon you. Or to put it another way: William Hurt may be lucky, but he certainly needs time.

"Hurt's talent is sturdy and momentarily saleable to a movie public that eats personalities for breakfast. Where the stage is concerned, however, he could not possibly be ready for all markets. . . . He has yet to make the big decisions, the ones that distinguish between poetry and prose, letting the ordinary speak through the verse and the remarkable sing out from the mundane. He looks alternately terrific—big-boned, sculptured, unself-consciously handsome—and lumpish, whitewashed, drab. The mix is not as volatile and attractive as it might be, no doubt because his presence is finally so indecisive." In the opinion of that writer, the kudos heaped upon Hurt were occurring prematurely. The great actors—Ralph Richardson, Michael Redgrave—saturated themselves in equally great works, usually the classics, while Hurt was rising above mediocre pieces. He had not been, felt that judge, adequately tested. "The young actor should be wary of fickle friends bearing hyperbolic gifts. Reviewers are surrogate salesmen. He, in his turn, is buying time to find something within his talent worth selling."

William Hurt was far from the only serious young actor to be lambasted for his apparently overnight success. His contemporaries, such as Meryl Streep, Sigourney Weaver, Al Pacino, and Robert De Niro, often managed to disturb reviewers having a bias toward the classics with their more modern attitude to performing. Not everyone wished to swallow the notion that a young actor could exude a strong physical presence that pleased audiences, while at the same time bring depth and validity to the characters he or she portrayed. Certainly the generation of actors who came to maturity during the sixties were educated in and respectful of the classics, but they believed that a complete repertoire demanded more. This generation valued the risks of experimentation, even though they might be stuck with a lemon every now and again. Now all major film actors, wealthy, powerful, yet still critically respected, time has proven Hurt and many of his peers right.

In Hurt's final television appearance, also in 1981, he co-starred with Sally Field (who had just won an Academy Award for *Norma Rae* and was winning respect for the first time in her lengthy career), in an adaptation of Tad Hosel's Pulitzer Prize–winning play, *All the Way Home.* The NBC broadcast was one of its rare live performances, and took place at the Bing Theater of the University of Southern California.

By the following summer, Hurt was back in New York, playing one of the few types of roles not yet associated with him—comedic. The actor, costumed "as a sort of Seneca Indian," in the words of New York *Post* critic Jerry Tallmer, appeared as Oberon in the Shakespeare Festival production of *A Midsummer Night's Dream.* A beloved tradition in New York, the Festival showcases some of the country's most acclaimed actors in open-air offerings that are free to the public. Joseph Papp, director of the program, is hailed as an innovative stylist who is unafraid to stage unconventional productions, and his *Dream* lived up to his reputation.

As Oberon, William Hurt made his entrances popping up from a hole in the ground. A female actress was cast as the elfin Puck, another departure from the norm. And although Tallmer was charmed by then eleven-year-old Emmanuel Lewis as a tiny changeling boy, he was less taken with Hurt. First defining the actor as a sex symbol, the critic then pointedly declared, "he is fine and dry and stoical at many key points. Sexual, I should say, he is not." Then again, Tallmer wasn't very thrilled with the entire production anyway.

In 1984, Hurt took a lengthy break from his catapulting film career to perform with an ensemble of equally famous stage and screen colleagues in David Rabe's vehement comedy drama, *Hurlyburly.* Following wintertime rehearsals in Chicago, the play was staged at the Promenade Theater; it moved to Broadway in August for a long, very successful run, although with several changes amongst the cast. Hurt, not surprisingly, played the pivotal role of Eddie, a Hollywood casting director whose own failures and weaknesses have dragged him down to a level where everyone else must suffer because of them. Eddie and his friends—played in the original company by Christopher Walken, Harvey Keitel, and Jerry Stiller—have little use for women, and blame their own disastrous relationships upon their hapless partners.

Because of Hurt's character's outright misogyny, many women found *Hurlyburly* a difficult play to enjoy, and even actress Sigourney Weaver was affected by the press of hostility that surrounded the troup. She explained, "The characters in this play are at each other's throats at some level. The play does not encourage cohesion. It puts you out there on the edge, and all kinds of dark feelings that are inside you come out when you're playing these roles."

At the same time, some actors discovered that their real-life feelings for one another could be used to positive effect. "I like Bill very much, so Mickey likes Eddie," said Christopher Walken. "Mickey's just like an extension of me. With me, acting depends a lot on how I feel, and on initial chemistry. I've been in things where there wasn't that much communication, but here, it was tremendous. . . . Certain people just add up to more than the sum of the individual parts."

And as the focal point for every other character, Hurt relished the opportunity he had to grow in the role. He viewed it as a process of steady involvement with and increased understanding of the part, and found the connections he needed from his colleagues. "I didn't know how to relate to anybody," he recalled. "Suddenly, I felt Chris (Walken) giving me this unbelievable energy. Our characters weren't talking to each other, there was no ostensible direct communication between them, and yet it became the most powerful thing in the scene for me, even though my job was not to look at him. I just felt it pouring down—the intelligence of it! It gave me a confidence, a physical impression; it was my first moment when I had a physical life onstage."

Since leaving *Hurlyburly,* William Hurt has been so involved with the demands of his film work that he has postponed returning to the stage for a while. However, its grueling requirements: bringing a character to life so that dozens, or hundreds, of performances will not dull its vitality; facing an audience that can love you or reject you, night after night; interacting with a company upon whom you must bestow total faith and trust—these things are too close to Hurt's own deep-seated needs as a performer and a person for him to shelve them indefinitely. Though he has found a wider circle, the theater will never be far from Hurt's mind, or his heart.

3

Altered States

JOURNEY TO THE CENTER OF A (PSYCHEDELIC) MIND

The movie business wanted William Hurt long before he was ready to throw in his lot with Hollywood. As is often the case with stage actors, Hurt was suspicious of the big screen's mechanisms—the ability to substitute a close-up for what must be verbalized, physically expressed emotions onstage. Also, the roles he was being offered didn't appeal to him. Too often, Hollywood relies on an endless replay of a particular season's one big hit, and Hurt was not an actor comfortable with spaceships, great white sharks, or haunted houses as replacements for an in-depth story line.

So when William Hurt read the script of *Altered States,* a new vista suddenly opened before him. He cried for forty-five minutes and "couldn't stand for another twenty," he told a *New York* magazine writer. "I was trying to express something in my own life, something I wanted so badly."

All the components of this movie seemed right to him. It was written by the legendary author Paddy Chayefsky, adapted from his novel. Chayefsky was an acknowledged master of several performing media, and his work showed a fundamental respect for the actor who would appear in it. Back in the early fifties, during the so-called "golden age of television," Chayefsky had written a play called *Marty,* which set a new standard for drama in this fledgling medium.

A poignant study of the relationship between a butcher and a shy, aging spinster, *Marty* was later adapted to the screen, where it won Oscars for best picture, best director, best actor and best screenplay. "With a sympathy rare among writers," observed one film historian, "Chayefsky observed the nuances of speech, the uncertain interplay of characters not brought up to command the world."

Throughout his lengthy career, Chayefsky excelled at capturing the heart of the underdog and popularized the honest environment surrounding his working-class protagonists. But in *Network,* the film he wrote directly before *Altered States,* Chayefsky created a most controversial document that bit the hand that had often fed him. In this movie, which also won an Oscar for best screenplay, Chayefsky denounced the very television industry which had given him a forum for some of his most acclaimed work. Through the eyes of the people it ruined—and in the rallying cry it prompted: "I'm mad as hell, and I'm not gonna take it anymore!"—the author judged television to be a spreader of poison, an industry where anything might be sacrificed for ratings, even people's lives. *Network* was a movie that prompted debates over its validity long after it had disappeared from the screen. And the kind of man who would turn his wrath on his supposedly benevolent master was an author whom a young, principled actor, tempted by the glamorous movie industry but still wary of its pitfalls, might relate to.

Similarly, the fact that *Altered States* was to be directed by Arthur Penn helped assure Hurt that he was making the right decision. Penn seemed an ideal choice for an actor grounded in the conventions and particular rewards of the theater. He was a triple threat—accomplished in directing for television and theater as well as film. (In fact, he had directed *The Miracle Worker* on television and on Broadway, and those successes enabled him to regain entrée to Hollywood after a four-year absence.)

The film that gained Penn his share of controversy, as well as a reputation as a visionary, was the mythic yet graphic *Bonnie and Clyde.* Offered the job by the film's producer-co-star, Warren Beatty, Penn rendered an unforgettable portrait of Depression-era America and the reckless desperation that might rule a person's life, making him or her do appalling things. While making no attempt to lessen the criminality of the outlaw couple, *Bonnie and Clyde* also humanized them: they were a troubled product of a troubled society. Not everyone bought the analogy, but in the turbulent sixties, a troubled society if ever there was one, it largely worked. "It is a simple story, brilliantly told," said one reviewer. "It does not tell the truth, but it works marvelously at that level where truth and legend meet—much better than in Penn's similar studies."

William Hurt was excited by the script of *Altered States,* but its filmmakers were also excited by him. Its producer, Howard Gottfried, ran into Hurt in an elevator, pronounced him a good actor, then stated, "We want to see you for Paddy Chayefsky's next film." The movie's executive producer, Daniel Melnick, had had Hurt touted to him by his niece, who shared an acting class with him, and by Penn. "I knew he had a certain quality when I saw the tape of *Verna: U.S.O. Girl,*" said Melnick. Hurt's initial meetings with Arthur Penn diminished his natural fear of starring in his first movie and heightened his expectations. He had dinner with the director and pronounced him "phenomenal."

The situation seemed ideal. However, *Altered States* was released in 1980, not in 1978, because for over a year the film degenerated into turmoil, leaving many of its principals to wonder if it would ever get off the ground. First, Arthur Penn became frustrated with the hallucinatory dimension of the movie and quit. Ken Russell—about as stylistically different from Penn as one could imagine—was called in as his replacement. Russell, a flamboyant personality, encountered immediate conflict with scriptwriter Chayefsky, who was a very visible presence on the set. Russell told writer Dan Yakir that he and Chayefsky had fundamental differences about the entire enterprise of filmmaking, which threw them into continuous crises. Said the British director, "I was a dancer years ago and I see the camera in terms of choreography—and he comes from the stage. He didn't understand what I was doing. He also talked to the actors without telling me, which is unforgivable."

After a week, Chayefsky was gone from the set. Distressed by its outcome, the renowned author substituted the pseudonym of Sidney Aaron for his own name for the scriptwriter credit.

Ken Russell had not been granted the accolades or critical esteem that had adhered to either Penn or Chayefsky. Yet another graduate of television, Russell had made his film debut in 1969 with an adaptation of D. H. Lawrence's *Women in Love.* It was immediately apparent to the film community that Russell had his own way of directing: the more outrageous, the better. As he increased his directing repertoire, Russell seemed curiously unaffected by the blunt criticisms he often received. Appalled by Russell's emphasis on violence and overt sexuality, some critics attacked his material as much as his directing style.

In a commentary dealing with his 1971 movie, *The Devils,* Russell was thoroughly damned as "lacking virtually every requirement of a filmmaker. He is capable of putting spectacular and outré images on the screen, but he has no gift for character, situation, pacing, rhythm, tension or tone." Yet Russell has never been willing to compromise his own visions, or tone down his flair for pyrotechnics. And if he had to work without favor, he decided, so be it. "Critics everywhere are very conservative," he explained. "I always think, 'Next time they'll be amazed—they'll surely see that this film has something.' But they don't, and you realize that it becomes a personal vendetta with quite a few of them."

Ordinarily, Russell wouldn't even have considered directing a project that was not his original idea, because he works only when there are certain qualities present. "All my films are about love, faith, sin, guilt, forgiveness and redemption," he has declared. However, two things prompted Russell to break with his own tradition and take over on *Altered States.* First, he was having no luck selling his next project and figured that this would be better than fading into oblivion. Second, he was initially interested in the film's subject matter, mind alteration, and enjoyed an increasing affinity with the material as his work progressed. Russell shaped the movie into meeting his criteria.

Meanwhile, already uneasy because of the chaos that swarmed around him, Hurt attempted to roll with the punches and fulfill his own expectations. A man with strong emotions and no qualms about expressing them, Hurt managed to keep the lid on while *Altered States* suffered through its upheavals. Primarily, Hurt worried about the result. Would it be the brilliant vision he had first detected in the screenplay, or an ill-conceived technicolor mess?

"Everybody's saying *big big big, major major major,* like in the Joseph Heller book," Hurt admitted to writer Cynthia Heimel back in 1979, when the film was still in production. "It's intimidating. But I have no reason to believe I won't get through this. My feet are on the ground. I'm going to have corns and sweat and stink and work. There's no reason to think, when I come back, that I'll be any different."

However, in retrospect, Hurt realized that the film's problems only compounded the worries he was facing as an actor about to explode into the general public's consciousness. "What was it going to be like?" he recalled. "If I wanted to walk down the street talking to myself, was it going to be reported in the New York *Post* the next day? Success can be nice, but it's also a strain. And there's a major concern: the thing you need in acting is concentration, and if one of the hazards of success is going to be distractions, well, that's a big subject."

Eventually, the shift in directors, the antagonism of the screenwriter, even the fact that there was a change in studios took its toll. "I have amnesia about that experience," Hurt revealed. "It was a hard time in my life—not one that I want to forget, but when you're living that intensely for that long a time, you tend to lose perspective. You don't understand it. You just show up every day and hold on for dear life.

"Have you ever been beaten up on the street? Well, working on a film set is easier," he wryly summed up his experience. At that point, few people were willing to predict whether *Altered States* was going to be a hit or a miss. All concerned were mainly relieved that, by 1980, it was finally over.

Altered States was made at a time when mind expansion and introspection were the furthest thing from the minds of the film audience. It was not a self-revelatory era, the time when Ronald Reagan was about to be elected president of the United States. Drugs such as LSD, and isolation chambers—the movie's departure point—were seen as the laughable product of the bygone age of hippies. American protagonists took two forms: the "new man"—tender, loving, and concerned for his partner's feelings, as typified by Alan Alda—was on his way out, being replaced by Clint Eastwood's "Dirty Harry" Callahan, whose word was the gun, and an all-American hero named Rocky. It did not seem an ideal time to focus on the obsessive mental journeys of the articulate, if emotionally explosive, preppy-looking character Hurt played, who belonged to neither of the dominant stereotypes. Yet in his role as college professor Eddie Jessup, William Hurt forced his audience to acknowledge that self-discovery in an isolation tank, and the visions it produced, were extremely important to them all.

The film, appropriately enough, begins in the psychedelic sixties, where Jessup takes his first trips in an isolation tank at college and senses that he is on the verge of a great discovery through his visions. Jessup's colleagues are willing to indulge his mania—after all, it's the sixties, and anything goes. But several years later, when Eddie, now a research scientist at Harvard, comes across a dusty isolation tank and resumes his inner-directed experiments, his friends are no longer so indulgent. Married to an anthropologist and the father of two children, Jessup starts to put his family in second place as his obsession with the tank increases. He believes that his visions are a key to man's earlier, prehuman state and is willing to risk everything for the answers.

Jessup enlarges upon these visions and discovers their hidden changes when he visits an Indian tribe in remote Mexico and shares in their hallucinogenic rituals. Despite the perils of challenging the unknown, he resumes his sessions in the tank, enhanced by the psychedelic herbs. His marriage a shambles, Jessup persists with the experiments, because he has felt his body begin to change and mutate into a nonhuman form. One night he stays in the tank long enough to metamorphose into an apelike creature, and he escapes into the city zoo, where he kills and devours a goat. By dawn, Jessup has returned to human form and manages to avoid discovery, but he has been permanently affected by the trip.

Staying away from the tank is no longer a guarantee that Jessup will remain in his human form. He unexpectedly begins to shift back on several occasions, barely stopping another catastrophic alteration. But his greatest test comes when, in his wife's presence, he experiences an almost complete reversion to an ultimate, prematter state of being. Terrified by the thought of losing the man she still loves, Emily Jessup risks her own life to save her husband, proving that the power of love is stronger than even the forces of eternity.

Much of this sometimes hard to believe movie is rooted in well-documented scientific research and anthropological observation. Psychedelic mushrooms have a history that extends as far back as prehistoric times. There is evidence that they were eaten by Vikings before they went into battle and were also used in ancient India to alter consciousness, to induce a state akin to the body control shown by some practitioners of yoga.

"Magic mushrooms," as the drug culture refers to them, are perhaps best known to North Americans from hundreds of years of use by the Indian cultures of Mexico. Reports of the effects of their visions are remarkably consistent, whether described by sixteenth-century Spanish conquistadors or visiting scientists four hundred years later. Wrote a Spanish monk, "They had another drunkenness which made them more cruel, which was of some small mushrooms . . . and after a while they were seeing a thousand visions, especially of snakes. And as they went completely out of their minds, it seemed to them that their legs and bodies were full of worms which were eating them alive. And thus half raving, they went out of the house wishing that somebody would kill them. . . ."

The later report noted that eating the mushrooms would "bring about a fission of the spirit, a split in the person, a kind of schizophrenia, with the rational side continuing to reason and to observe sensations that the other side is enjoying." However, even a modern, rational person runs the risk of losing his more balanced side without proper guidance. One report from a remote Mexican town told of an American who ingested the mushrooms on his own and tried to eat a live turkey during his trip. Such overwhelming confusion between the imagination and reality are totally consistent with Eddie Jessup's bizarre hallucinations of lizards, visions of hell, and of him and his wife as a kind of Sphinx, eroding away into dust.

The Indians of Mexico used psychedelic mushrooms to assist them in their religious ceremonies, but modern man seems constantly on the prowl for new methods of altering his consciousness. The heightened body experience is sought not only by the drug addict, looking for new ways to escape reality, but has also been felt by astronauts, who found that they could actually see dirt roads and streetlights as they circled the globe a hundred miles out in space. In between the unexpected vision and the numbing-out experience is a wide range of methods by which the mind can be altered. It can result from hypnosis, sleep, anesthesia, biofeedback, seizures, fasting, meditation, sex, dancing, and even weightlessness. Perhaps most fascinating and tantalizing are the reports of those people who were actually judged dead for several minutes, only to rejoin the living and describe the strange lights and images they insisted belonged to the other side.

Scientists, too, encourage the kind of mind altering Eddie Jessup achieved when they seek joining points between humans and our apelike ancestors. Since we evolve along an unbreakable time line, surely it's not in error to assume that somewhere, in the backs of our minds, a shard of collective memory of that long-ago era might still exist. Such a link with the continuity and oneness of life is at the heart of meditation, an altered state of mind so accepted that it has been judged a valid state of being, just like awareness, sleep, and dreaming.

Throughout the twentieth century, respected scientists experimented with mind altering drugs and other devices to test their theories of what constitutes reality. In 1929, British psychiatrist William James experimented with peyote, a component of the mushroom, and nitrous oxide, the so-called "laughing gas" used today in thousands of dental offices. He wrote that surrounding "our normal waking consciousness, parted from it by the filmiest of screens, there lie potential forms of consciousness entirely different."

Twenty-five years later, Aldous Huxley, a writer as well as a scientist, took mescaline pills and felt "the doors of perception", as he titled the book about his experiences, opening to admit a different level of reality. The scientific community slowly began to explore different realities unearthed in foreign cultures, while continuing limited research with psychedelics at home. Timothy Leary, a Harvard psychologist, transformed his life when he ate psychedelic mushrooms in Mexico in 1960. Within a few years, Leary had taken his quest for ultimate enlightenment to his students, as they took a manufactured psychedelic, LSD-25, and studied their hallucinations. Of course, the widespread unguided use of such powerful mind-altering chemicals resulted in their being declared illegal by 1966.

However, before legal LSD experimentation was completely curtailed, John Lilly began a series of mental adventures using the drug in combination with an isolation tank. The isolation tank is filled with water, precisely temperature controlled to match blood heat, and is kept in total darkness. When the user floats on the surface of the water, with the tank closed overhead, he or she receives absolutely no stimulation from the outside. Invariably, one's thoughts turn inward. Lilly, a physician and psychoanalyst with training in neurophysiology, biology, and electronics, was operating under a grant from the National Institute of Mental Health, which had allowed him the LSD. What he planned to study under such extreme conditions were pathological states of consciousness. He realized that even a healthy person might, under the right conditions, slip into those states, perhaps with terrifying results.

He wrote, "It wasn't bodily death that I feared. It was getting into spaces in which I would lose control and from which I would perhaps not be able to come back." Despite the risk, he let himself be carried into new areas of consciousness, which to him became just as real as the waking state. "I moved into universes containing beings much larger than myself," he observed. "The first time I entered these spaces, I was swept, pushed, carried, whirled and in general beat around by processes which I could not understand, processes of immense energy, of fantastic light, and of terrifying power." And sometimes, when he felt himself losing control over his fundamental senses, Lilly forced himself to return to his body before the choice was taken away.

Lilly's experiments became the basis of body-mind alteration using isolation tanks. Even without the extra stimulation of hallucinogenic drugs, participants in isolation tank studies revealed that, with no grounding in our normal sensory world, their minds often took them into different worlds. For some, it was invigorating, for others, horrific.

Director Ken Russell saw the yearnings of Eddie Jessup for absolute truth as a Pandora's box, "which he opens, trying to get to the unfathomable. His sin—his presumptuousness, arrogance and blindness—is far greater and more universal than that of the artists I explored," said the director, speaking of his biographical films about Mahler, Tchaikovsky, and Liszt.

In the eyes of Hurt's costars, the role of Eddie Jessup suited him perfectly. Though Hurt takes great pains to avoid being confused with his characters—"That's not acting, it's schizophrenia," he has said in many ways, at many times—in *Altered States,* certain similarities between man and role could not be ignored. "Bill *is* Eddie," stated Blair Brown, who played the role of Emily Jessup, his long-suffering wife. "He's an adventurer with people and emotions, a truly brave man who plunges ahead even when he doesn't quite know what he's doing."

Typical of Hurt's complete immersion in his parts was the way he got to know his costar, Bob Balaban, who played one of Jessup's main assistants, Arthur Rosenberg. Learning that Balaban would be portraying his character's close friend in the film, Hurt showed up unexpectedly at the actor's apartment, wanting to get to know him. When Balaban's wife told Hurt that her husband wasn't home, he said that he'd wait. He did—for six hours. Said Balaban, "Eddie Jessup is a character who's driven and obsessed with the desire to find a perfect truth. There's a strong core of that in Bill. In his acting, he's a person who's striving all the time. He sometimes drives himself crazy with that, but he's always trying to be the best actor he can."

Having committed himself to starring in *Altered States,* having survived the clash of titanic personalities that made the set an uncertain landscape as weeks passed, Hurt was still unsure of the final result. To one questioner, he appeared to support his director: "I heard people say about Ken Russell that he is crazy and he hurts people. It seemed to me he had a lively imagination and he is honestly and passionately going after his work."

However, several months before the film's release, to another person he did not come off nearly as optimistic. "I haven't seen it," he revealed, "but I'll be surprised if it has any kind of performance in it. I signed for it because Arthur Penn was the original director. He's a sensitive artist who has dedicated his career to American lyricism. Then he dropped out and was replaced by Ken Russell, an Englishman, who has devoted his career to the destruction of style. I just did what I was told," the actor dispiritedly declared.

The critics, long willing to throw barbs at Russell, had a field day when *Altered States* was released on Christmas Day, 1980. This was a film of extremes, with great gasps of color, light, and sound, and not much time for reflection until it had survived its climax. Consequently, the traditionalists hated it, and the visionaries, if they weren't willing to allow it full points due to its excesses, at least gave it an E for effort.

The *Daily News*, in giving the film two stars, pointed out that "it has been directed with a great flourish by Ken Russell who, as usual, is far more interested in playing around with the visual effects than in developing flesh-and-blood characters. . . . The characters, in particular the ego-tripping Jessup, behave so ludicrously and they remain such stuffy academic types that it is impossible to care what happens to them." Janet Maslin, writing in *The New York Times*, was slightly more generous, though she perceived the irreconcilable incompatibility between Russell and Chayefsky. "It's easy to guess why he and Mr. Russell didn't see eye to eye. The direction, without being mocking or campy, treats outlandish material so matter-of-factly that it often has a facetious ring. The screenplay, on the other hand, cries out to be taken seriously, as it addresses, with no particular sagacity, the death of God and the origins of man.

"The film is in fine shape as long as it revels in its own craziness, making no claims on the viewer's reason. But when it asks you to believe that what you're watching may really be happening, and to wonder what it means, it is asking far too much."

But for *Time*'s critic Richard Corliss, "Too much here is just enough." Fed up with a spate of simplistic films, in which brutal actions spoke much louder than the few words that were exchanged, Corliss relished a movie that relied on "verbal and sensory overload." He wanted a movie that was more than a meaningless walk-through, and recognized the transcendance of a good science fiction picture that was also a satisfying love story. (Interestingly, in 1986, when Canadian filmmaker David Cronenberg remade *The Fly*, fusing an extremely graphic horror movie with a love story, it too prompted conflicting reactions. Condemned to an even greater degree than was *Altered States, The Fly* was praised by those few perceptive writers who recognized the ultimate risks one lover may have to face without abandoning their partner.)

Wrote Corliss, "The movie is also, and ultimately, Russell's. From William Hurt he got . . . a star performance of contorted intensity, mandarin charm and sleek sensuality. Russell's direction of actors and camera has never been so cagey, so controlled, so alive to the nuances of language and personality. . . . Russell has devised a film experience that will astound some viewers, outrage others, and bore nobody. Laugh with it, scream at it, think about it. You may leave the theater in an altered state." Quite a different point of view from the *News*'s Kathleen Carroll, who, misinterpreting Hurt's empathy with the role, dealt him this backhanded compliment: "William Hurt plays Jessup with total conviction and the fact that he could do so with such a straight face shows what a fine actor he really is."

Several reviewers saw *Altered States* as an analogy, adapted from myth or religion. *Newsweek*'s David Ansen, who praised the film as "an outrageous and chilling entertainment," viewed the relationship between Eddie and Emily Jessup as a retelling of the Orpheus-Eurydice legend, in which Emily must rescue her Orpheus from hell. However, both Corliss and *New York* magazine critic David Denby believed that the film referred to Jesus and Mary. Wrote Denby, "When Blair Brown, as Jessup's wife, takes the naked, mutilated Hurt into her arms, we are meant to think of the moment as Mary's receiving Christ's body—a modern Pietà. The movie is full of this pious, slightly masochistic eroticism."

With the weight of celebrity about to descend on him in full force, being described as Christlike must have made Hurt feel even more disoriented. Certainly, the actor was intense, committed to the ideal of good theater, introspective, and deeply motivated by his craft. But he wasn't about to stand up and urge anyone to follow him. In fact, as Hurt has become internationally idolized, he draws a strict line between his public image and his private self. "I shouldn't be standing up on a soapbox in another area," he once said. "I shouldn't be mixing my metaphors. I shouldn't be into politics because I got famous as an actor. I still have my own ideas but I shouldn't be taking advantage of my position because it would dilute my acting and it would dilute politics and it would dilute myself to do it. Those areas are not areas where I am prepared to take the same risks."

Hurt's recognition far outweighed the mixed reviews

given to his debut film. One writer might have noticed his "poignantly expressive" eyes, another his athletic body, and yet another, his mental acuity. The verdict on William Hurt was in: "Hurt is brilliantly cast," said *Newsweek*'s Ansen. "With his blond, brutal Wasp good looks, his cold compuslive rhythms, he's totally believable as a maverick Harvard intellectual, but his pleading, loony eyes draw you into his torment." In *Altered States,* William Hurt redefined the role of the obsessive truth-seeker in modern terms. He made total commitment to an ideal—even an unpopular one—a state worthy of admiration and empathy.

4

Eyewitness

A MURDER MYSTERY WITH HEART AND SOUL

Altered States had completed filming but was still over a year from being released when William Hurt became connected with his second film role. He had returned to New York and was very content rehearsing for *Hamlet* with his colleagues at the Circle Rep. His first foray into filmmaking had ended up putting the actor into the middle of a battle zone, and at this point, Hurt couldn't predict whether he'd been seen as a talent or an incompetent. Unlike the theater, in which a part was thoroughly his, a film was basically taken out of his hands once the shoot was over. Under control of the director and editor, an actor may achieve a far different result than what he had intended.

Although accomplished in his theatercraft, when it came to film Hurt remained somewhat uncomfortable with the medium and the abruptness of the environment. "I feel like I'm in kindergarten," he confessed. "I'm embarrassed by all I don't know. But acting is acting and movies just require more patience. When I finish a film I get a wrenching feeling when people finish up and go away. In the theater, it's more like a family and you know they'll be back tomorrow night." He was being touted as a luminous presence and deluged with scripts for his follow-up project. Hurt refused most of them after perusing a few pages. "I've got to believe in what

I'm doing and most films are just junk," he declared. "When they talk about intelligence as being a barrier to good acting, that makes me cringe. Those people want puppets. I really like to act and want to be proud of what I do."

Therefore, when the director-writer team of Peter Yates and Steve Tesich came along with their new film, titled at that time *The Janitor Doesn't Dance,* Hurt was delighted to accept the leading role, Daryll Deever, a loner who unwittingly gets drawn into a world of intrigue, love, and murder. "We were looking for a person whose sincerity was believable," said director Yates. "Bill has an incredible vulnerability, yet I felt he was able to portray the essential quality of Daryll—that is, a man who's come to grips with his life."

Even as he was still learning the ropes about film acting, Hurt knew that the ultimate strength or weakness of a movie depended on the quality of the script and the ability of the director. After his first experience, in which both underwent extreme changes, Hurt devised a set of personal guidelines that he consistently referred to when considering a part. Money and sex appeal, by the way, weren't on that list. The actor was exclusively concerned with those factors that built up, or that might damage, his own performing ethic.

"It's basically a hunch," he explained, "an informed hunch based on any number of things. I always choose on the basis of the strength of the screenplay and the compatibility I feel I may have with the director. He informs me about a situation he plans and, if that works with me, great. It's mainly how good I think the screenplay is. I don't break things down in terms of what's special about my character. My character, per se, is not the most important thing.

"As cynical as we can get about it, I still believe that people are created equal, so anything well-written which is not about the standardization and homogenization of man but about equality, is important to me. Any destruction of a stereotype is important." *The Janitor,* which would retain that title in Europe but was renamed *Eyewitness* in the United States, satisfied all of those conditions. The product of a successful, well-respected collaborative team, it gave new depth to potentially stereotypical characters and restructured that tried and true cinematic genre, the murder mystery, into a new world that included personal politics and the force of human emotions.

Peter Yates, a British-born director, made a fairly smooth transition from his homeland to the U.S., where he has been working since the late sixties. Yates had been directing crime stories abroad and made a strong impact with his first American project, the 1968 *Bullitt,* co-starring Steve McQueen and Robert Vaughn. The film was a smash for which car chase aficionados show great reverence—this was the movie that began the seemingly endless profusion of high-speed automobile careening. His follow-up, a relationship movie called *John and Mary,* which starred then newcomer icons Dustin Hoffman and Mia Farrow, was poorly received, and for several years Yates was not a name that readily came to mind when discussing directorial greats.

All that changed when, in the late seventies, Yates teamed up with a young screenwriter named Steve Tesich, who had created a tale based on his adolescence in the Midwest. It was a classic coming-of-age adventure: four working-class boys are rivals to a pack of more privileged youth in the town of Bloomington, Indiana. Their test of combat here was a bicycle race, which is won in true *Rocky* style by the underdog heroes. Though the outcome was predictable, both critics and the public responded to the charm of *Breaking Away,* which was leavened by a good chunk of mirth—a necessity if this type of movie isn't going to be labeled a tedious morality play. Wrote one critic, "Tesich is at least humorous with it—and since his humor is, if not original, likeable, and since Yates approaches it in the manner of Capra rather than say, Blake Edwards (whose humor is of a much darker hue), all is permissible."

Breaking Away won the hearts of its audience and unexpectedly became an Academy Award winner. Attention was therefore focused of the men who brought it to life, and everyone waited to see what Yates and Tesich might do next. News that they were working together on their next project may have led some to expect another heartwarming, upbeat project. *Eyewitness* was about as different as could be imagined, though both director and writer would rely on their own unique abilities to form this film—Yates on his affinity for detailed locations, and Tesich for his autobiographical flavoring.

Eyewitness centers around a janitor who works late at night in an office building, apparently content with his lot in life. A Vietnam veteran, he seems relatively unscathed by that experience, except for his senses, which are extremely acute and which he tests often, engaging in mock trial-by-combat with his ferocious-looking pet dog. Daryll Deever, the janitor, has a best friend named Aldo—whom Vietnam did mentally scar for life—and a girlfriend, Aldo's sister, who he dutifully beds but seems curiously uninvolved with. The person of Deever's heart, however, is someone he's never met, a confident-sounding television reporter named

Tony Sokolow. The daughter of wealthy East European Jews, Tony switches between the blood-spattered world of crime stories and her parents' upper-class, cultured circle. Her fiancé is dedicated to a noble cause, the freeing of Soviet Jews.

Daryll and Tony appear unlikely ever to cross paths. She is completely unaware of his existence, though he is obsessed with hers. Every night after work, Deever rushes home and immerses himself in videotapes of her broadcasts. Of course, their paths do cross one day. Working alone at his cleaning chores, the janitor discovers that a Vietnamese diamond importer has been murdered right in his office. Along with the police come the reporters and camera crews, and Deever realizes that this is the opportunity he's been longing for. He intimates that he has some information about the crime, which brings Tony and her associates running. Daryll soon admits that he's really interested in her, but keeps her interest piqued by maintaining that he does have newsworthy tidbits. Despite her problem-free personal life, Tony finds herself falling for the amiable yet inner-directed janitor.

Eventually the lovers find their relationship endangered by the murder Daryll witnessed, and the threat of death begins to tighten around both of them. Only by risking everything they've built together and defying the system that would otherwise split them apart do Daryll and Tony win the right to be together. The cost, however, is more than either of them, especially Tony, could ever have imagined.

Typical of a Tesich screenplay, the author strongly identifies with his hero and incorporated some of his own experiences into Daryll. "While I was in college," Tesich explained, "I spent four of my summer vacations working as a night janitor in Chicago. It was an ideal job for someone who wanted to be a writer because it lent itself to all sorts of fantasies. Just being in a building late at night all alone, you would begin to fantasize about what might be happening on the other floors and behind the locked doors. You could actually enter some of the shops and offices because you had the master keys.

"Your imagination was always playing tricks. The air-conditioning would suddenly kick off and scare the hell out of you. It was a strange, eerie night world," Tesich said. "No one else was supposed to be in the building. Yet you would hear things, sounds echoing through the corridors, and wonder who was doing what. Unlike Daryll, I never discovered a body, but there were times when I half expected to. I knew I would have to write about it, and I knew it would make the perfect setting for a murder mystery."

Strangely enough, the writer also suffered from an obsession—fortunately, a fairly innocuous one—with a well-known female television journalist. He confessed, "For some reason, I have no idea why, I developed this all-consuming fascination for Lesley Stahl, the CBS Washington correspondent. If I'd had one of those video recorders, I would have been just like Daryll, recording the news every night just to watch her over and over again.

"I used to see her on the screen and wonder what that woman did when she wasn't standing there in front of the White House. I'd wonder just how far I would go in order to meet her. Would I commit a crime, or would I claim to have information about a crime, just to have the privilege of being interviewed by her and, perhaps, getting to know her?"

There is more to *Eyewitness,* however, than love and

death. Tesich also considered the problems of class conflict, which he had introduced in *Breaking Away*. The contrast between Daryll Deever, with his janitor's jumpsuit, motorcycle, and walk-up apartment, and Tony's designer clothes and exquisitely furnished home, is painful. Deever, as a true egalitarian hero, isn't taken aback by the privileges of others; instead, he takes the advantage. "Say, your floors need buffing or anything?" he teases Tony upon first visiting her apartment, in a provocative sexual tone worthy of Mae West. Tesich's working-class hero is a man who can handle both things and people, a man who tragedy toughens.

Tesich and Yates went for quality, not proven box-office bonanza, when they cast the leading roles in *Eyewitness*. At that time, William Hurt was still an unknown to film audiences, though his theatrical and television performances had won numerous accolades. His long, lean costar, Sigourney Weaver, wasn't exactly a household word yet, either. She, however, had made her film debut, as the tough-minded female astronaut who is the only survivor in the science fiction epic, *Alien*—not exactly a fitting prerequisite for a central character in a love story. Both women did show strength under pressure, and that attracted Weaver, who had trained at the Yale drama school, to the role. Like Hurt, she too was ready to reject roles that weren't, as she put it, "meat and potatoes." Almost six feet tall, with a face that carved itself into strong expressions, Weaver wasn't about to accept any parts intended for Suzy Homemaker.

"It's a film of conflicting views," Sigourney Weaver believed. "The reality of the woman. The impression created by the media personality. Daryll's romanticized view of her. Her parents' image of her. And the point of view of the film itself, which constantly crisscrosses. You're never sure who she is.

"Tony comes from a refined, cultured family. She could have a career as a classical musician, but she gets a job in hard news, which goes against her parents' expectations. She's enigmatic; that's why I wanted to play her."

The film's supporting cast, which included Christopher Plummer as Tony's suave fiancé and James Woods as Daryll's troubled friend, reinforced the company's feeling that they were making a movie of quality. That kind of meticulous attention to detail didn't end when *Eyewitness* finished casting. That was just one out of many rigors both cast and crew would willingly go through to make a successful production.

Both Hurt and Weaver wanted to create authentic characters, and consequently spent lengthy preparation time familiarizing themselves with Daryll's and Tony's life-styles. Sigourney Weaver put in several weeks' time accompanying a TV news crew on their story-gathering rounds, while William Hurt worked the all-night cleaning shift in the Empire State Building. Both found their experiences to be revelatory.

"I was surprised to see how successful women reporters are," commented Weaver. "In fact, I think they have an edge over their male colleagues because they can be terribly charming and exude the kind of personality that makes people want to talk and open up.

"I also discovered that women reporters are always being sent to cover the grisly stories. Every time to you see a close-up of blood on the subway platform, there will usually be a blonde with a microphone standing there. I find that kind of sexual assigning hard to take sometimes," the rangy actress admitted, "but I guess the news directors feel that having a 'delicate' creature in a tough environment makes for a better show." Well, Tony may have been one of the fairer sex, but as played by Weaver, the fairer sex couldn't be assumed to be the weaker one. Still, after her role in *Alien,* which included a great deal of improvising and physical action, Weaver was delighted to be working with an expertly written, fully fleshed-out script.

As far as William Hurt was concerned, *Eyewitness* gave him the opportunity to put some of his personal talents to work, things that came as a complete surprise to Peter Yates after he cast Hurt in the role of Deever. Hurt pointed out that he had ridden across the country on a motorcycle and had been an accomplished horseman since childhood, both skills that he was called upon to use in his part. "I'm practically a stuntman," joked the athletic actor.

But spending an intensive period of rehearsal time as a janitor gave him a new perspective on what some people might demean as manual labor. "I spent time with a janitor who was a waxer, which is la crème de la crème of the profession. I had thought that maybe Daryll was overqualified for his job, but the point is, the great thing about him is that he's *not.* He has self-respect and respect for other people. He doesn't believe he's better than anyone else or any worse. He feels he's the equal of anyone, and that's what allows him to ignore the class distinction between himself and Tony and actively pursue her." Hurt feels strongly about the need for respect, as given to all types of people, which is why he has always tended to downplay the star status of his life. "What I respect about Bill is that he's not afraid to sound like an asshole," said Sigourney Weaver, who remained friendly with Hurt after their film together was ended and acted with him onstage several years later in *Hurlyburly.*

One final component remained to make *Eyewitness* an authentic mood piece, rather than simply another cops and bad guys tale—details. Director Yates had been praised for his attention to detail in calling up the midwestern landscapes of *Breaking Away.* In *Eyewitness,* which pulls so many different ethnic groups and cultures into its milieu, Yates made its New York location work for him. The director combed New York in search of the right buildings to use to suit each family's level of wealth, then meticulously decorated his establishments, at one point bringing in a lace tablecloth to add the right touch to Tony's parents' apartment.

"I know of no other city in the world that would close down one of its major bridges just to let us shoot on it," Yates enthused to columnist Rex Reed. "I've tried to make New York look different. It's usually shown as a Jewish or Italian town, but the city will be more cosmopolitan in this film. It's a city of enormous contrast, a mixture of different architectures and different languages and I've used them all. Sigourney plays a girl who comes from wealthy Jewish immigrants, Bill comes from an Irish middle-class family in Queens, Plummer is from Israel. They could only come together in New York." Locations such as a little known mansion on Fourteenth Street and the Claremont Riding Stables on the Upper West Side helped Yates to reach his aim of "a polished look."

If the turmoil surrounding his first picture had given William Hurt cause to fear for his place in the medium, *Eyewitness* prompted just the opposite response. This was the kind of ensemble production that Hurt knew best and was comfortable working within. He and his colleagues were allowed—encouraged, in fact—to take ample preparation time for their characters to mesh. Egos were sublimated to a higher purpose, a cohesive film. Hurt extolled Yates as a man "who truly enjoys actors. When I was on his set I felt I was one of the crew. I can get just as tickled watching a set decorator go at making a room. I can cry watching it. It gives me a thrill, that sort of skill."

Eyewitness, at three times the budget of the surprise hit *Breaking Away,* did not match its predecessor's revenues or, unfortunately, its box office receipts. Because it was more than a one-dimensional crime story, it may have befuddled some viewers. However, the critics tended to treat it more kindly, praising the film's eccentricity and originality, even if they weren't about to hand over an unqualified rave. Writing in *The New York Times,* Vincent Canby covered all sides of the issue by labeling *Eyewitness* "a thoroughly delightful but far from plausible mystery melodrama that operates exclusively on high spirits and a no-nonsense intelligence that is never sidetracked by coherence. . . . Daryll Deever is probably one of the dimmest characters to be seen in any first-rate movie in years, but something happens in Mr. Hurt's performance to make him not only credible, but also important. He's funny. He's sensitive. He's logical (even when the movie is not)."

New York magazine's critic, David Denby, was far more upbeat in his assessment, pronouncing the film "completely enjoyable and fresh. . . . Both men [Tesich and Yates] use the thriller form to open life up rather than narrow it down; they put into the movie their feelings about romantic fantasy and friendship, their knowledge of how American class relationships work. *Eyewitness* isn't neat or disciplined or ruthlessly suspenseful; it's a wry, funny, slightly rumpled and ruminative movie, with the scary highs spaced out among the many moments of gentle observation."

Ironically, *Eyewitness* opened its run in February, 1981, only a few weeks after Hurt's controversial debut project, *Altered States.* The two films emerged as polar opposites—one subtle, the other a screaming frenzy. And William Hurt, in the leading roles of both, proved that he was not the kind of actor one could easily typecast. All Daryll Deever and Eddie Jessup had in common were their obsessions, but even those were singular: in one case, a dream lover, in the other, the basic truth about the origins of the cosmos. Whether playing it expansive or close to the vest, Hurt stood out like a beacon. And even he was becoming excited about what this medium might do for his art.

"*Eyewitness* is only my second movie, and it's been a joy for me," Hurt said with elation. "*Altered States,* because it was my first film, was my baptism by fire. It was like climbing a mountain. When you get back from the peak, you're not sure that the fact that you lost three toes to frostbite made it worth it to reach the top. Now I think it was. I feel like I'm going to be around for a long time."

William Hurt's courageous role as a flagrant homosexual in *Kiss of the Spider Woman* won him an Oscar as Best Actor of 1985. Proudly displaying their trophies along with Hurt are Anjelica Huston, Best Supporting Actress, and Geraldine Page, Best Actress. *(Vinnie Zuffante/Star File)*

After completing *Children of a Lesser God,* Hurt took some time off to relax, which included sprouting a luxurious beard. Actually, Hurt wore a beard when he made his TV debut on "Kojak" at the very start of his career. *(Walter McBride/Retna Ltd.)*

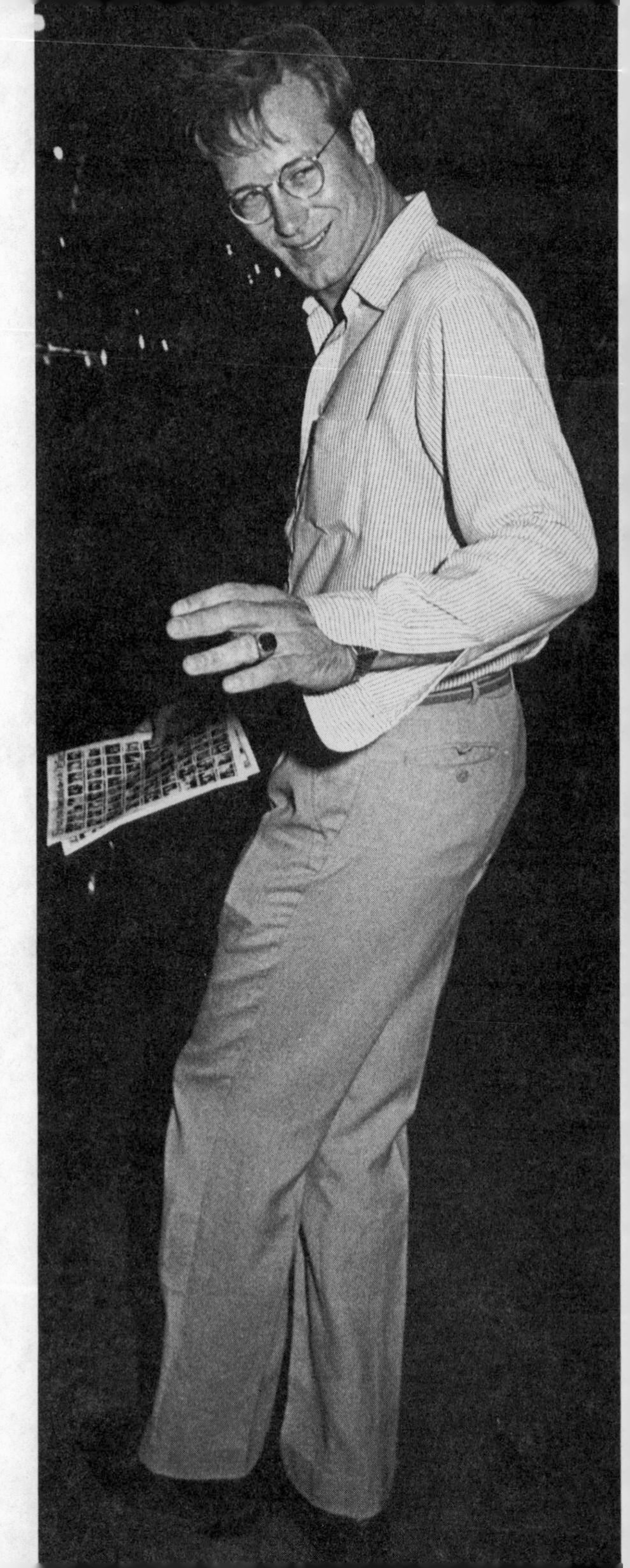

A candid moment as the actor is pursued by photographers after a performance of *Hurlyburly*, in which he appeared on Broadway with an all-star ensemble cast. *(Ron Galella)*

Hot newcomer Laura Dern (daughter of actor Bruce Dern) welcomed friends such as William Hurt to a party in honor of her film, *Smooth Talk.* The February 1986 bash was held at renowned New York nightspot Area. *(Anthony Savignano/Galella Ltd.)*

Though unpredictable in his behavior with the press, William Hurt graciously responds to an autograph request from an obviously enthralled fan.
(Ron Galella)

A rare shot of the actor with Sandra Jennings, the ballet dancer who was his constant companion for several years and is the mother of his son, Alex.
(Ron Galella)

In the award-winning *Kiss of the Spider Woman*, Raul Julia's revolutionary Valentin and William Hurt's window dresser Molina taught each other much about life . . . and love.

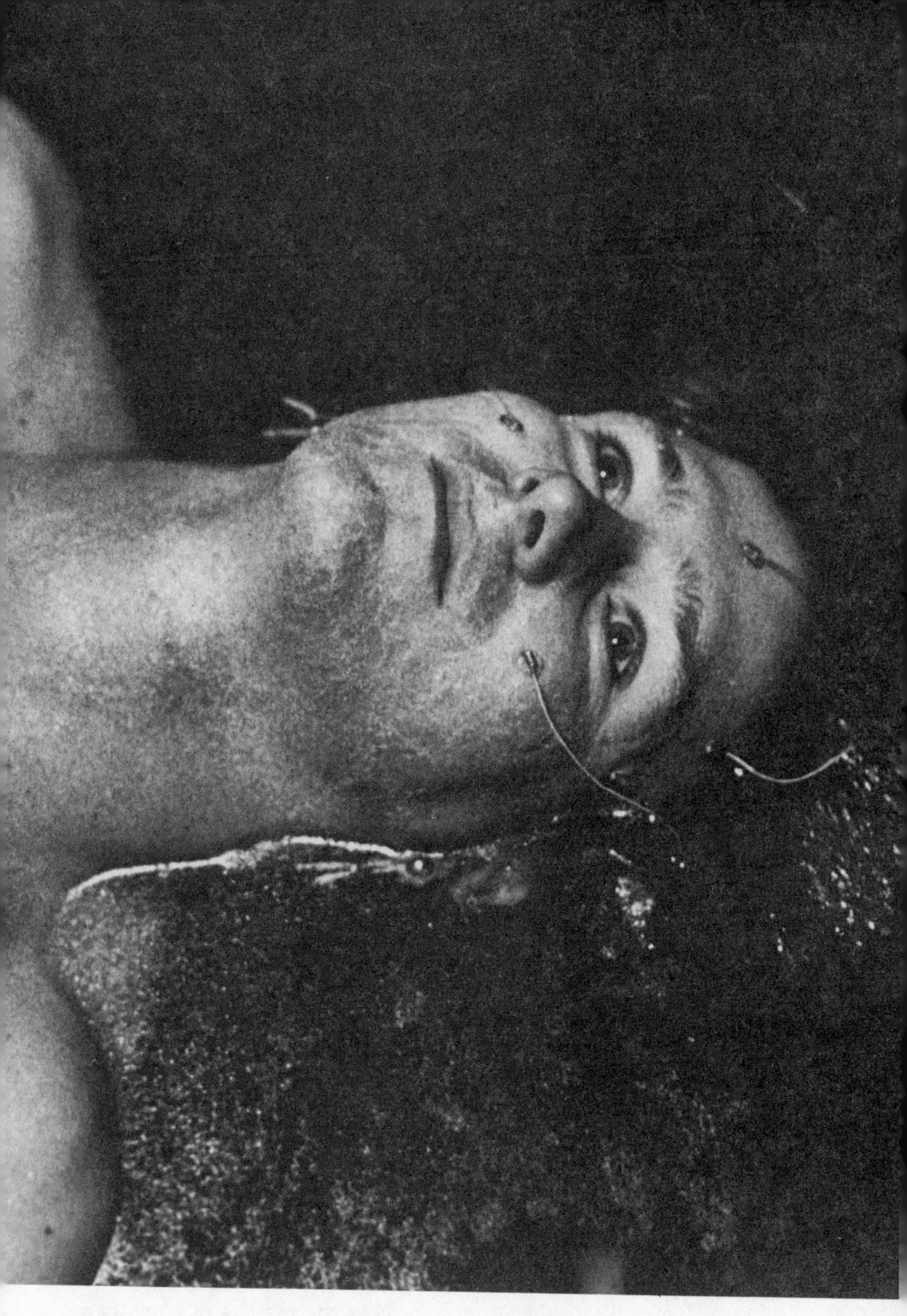

An attention-getting debut. As the star of *Altered States,* William Hurt showed the movie-going public the passions that lurked beneath his all-American exterior.

While playing onscreen lovers in *Children of a Lesser God*, William Hurt and his young costar, Marlee Matlin, fell in love.

Those striking WASP good loo
led the readers of *Good Housekeepi*
to name William Hu
"sexiest man" of the yea

Despite the attention given him for leading roles,
Hurt has always preferred to work with talented peers.
Some critics have held that the spectacular cast of *The Big Chill*
was better than the film itself.
From left: JoBeth Williams, Jeff Goldblum, Mary Kay Place,
Tom Berenger, William Hurt, Meg Tilly, Glenn Close, and Kevin Kline.

As Ned Racine, a lawyer looking for kicks, William Hurt was lured into a devastating affair with Kathleen Turner's vamp, Matty Walker, in the 1981 film *Body Heat.*

Eyewitness linked Hurt with
then-newcomer Sigourney Weaver,
in a complex tale that was
part romance, part murder mystery,
and part psychological case study.

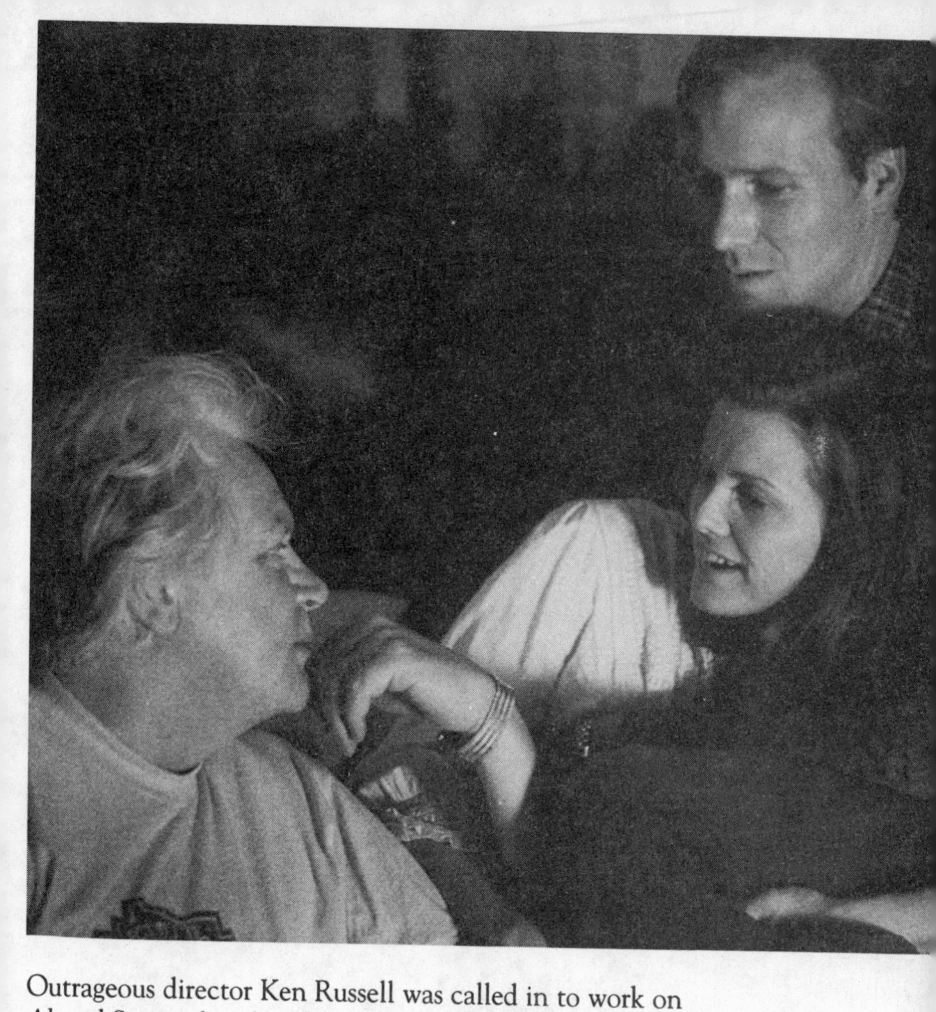

Outrageous director Ken Russell was called in to work on *Altered States* after the film ran into problems.
This resulted in more chaos when screenwriter Paddy Chayefsky abruptly resigned.
Shown with Russell and Hurt is Blair Brown, who played Emily Jessup, the long-suffering wife of Hurt's Eddie Jessup.

(Next page)You'd never guess, to see their casual attire and relaxed attitudes, that Kathleen Turner and William Hurt conducted an incendiary onscreen relationship in *Body Heat.*
(Richard Young/Retna Ltd.)

5

Body Heat

WILLIAM HURT GETS VERY PHYSICAL

"I am a character man in a leading man's body," William Hurt declared to *The New York Times* just before *Body Heat,* his third film to be issued within nine months, was released. "I love character roles. I'm trained for them. I have much more fun playing them." Before his first forays into Hollywood, Hurt was able to conceive of himself as an ensemble player. Although he had starred in many of his stage roles, he was a member of a company. No one inside that circle treated him any differently. And Hurt had decided, almost from the start, not to read his own press reviews. What purpose could they serve? he asked himself. Only to inflate, or possibly deflate, his ego, according to what prevailing opinion dictated, and not be of much assistance in polishing his craft. For the same reason, he went out of his way to avoid interviews with reporters, preferring to let his parts speak for themselves.

This somewhat insular attitude was why he had stayed in New York, resisting the screen's siren call. For other actors, the reluctance to declare oneself a leading man might be construed as self-protection, an effective backup device if the top-drawer roles never came. In the case of William Hurt, however, his wariness soon had a solid cause. Once *Body Heat* hit America's movie theaters, inflaming an already hot summer of 1981, Hurt was declared a leading man and a sex symbol. To a man who was attempting to live a somewhat normal life, sharing an Upper West Side apartment with an American Ballet Theatre dancer named Sandra Jennings, studhood was not in the preferred scheme of events. He would, nonetheless, have to get used to it.

"He is a Wasp heartthrob on whose chest the Lacoste alligator shirt was meant to be displayed," gushed the *Times* in an unlikely feast of fandom. "This blond, hunky six-footer will be the Wasp movie idol of the eighties," predicted *Time* magazine. "He brought a scary sexuality to the traditional Wasp prototype," commented *Newsweek*. Articles were accompanied by bare-chested photos of the actor, or partially clad shots that featured his riveting pale blue eyes. A new-age icon, for the dreamers unmoved by dark, ethnic types or bulky bodybuilders, was alive and well—even if none of this was the actor's intent. By opening himself up to passionate love scenes in his first two films—movies that also put the actor's unclad contours on frequent display—Hurt had unwittingly set the context for his popularity. But when the graphic, violent sexual tone of *Body Heat* further fleshed out the image, despite himself, Hurt's reluctance to play along was swept away. He was that most elusive fantasy figure—the man who is generous with his body but still keeps tantalizing secrets locked into his mind. William Hurt became one of the rarest types of movie images: an uninhibited, sexual person with a brain as relentless and probing as more obvious parts of his anatomy.

Body Heat has been debated since its release by the critical community. Some have praised its calculating brilliance and frank presentation, while others disdained it as merely calculating and exploitative. Whatever was said, the film was and still is an instant attention-getter. As much as calling attention to its principal players, William Hurt and Kathleen Turner, the movie announced that its director-writer, then thirty-two-year-old Lawrence Kasdan, had to be reckoned with as a new, hot Hollywood titan.

William Hurt's previous efforts had been placed in the hands of veteran British directors, and in the case of *Altered States,* a legendary screenwriter. Larry Kasdan, on the other hand, was barely a year older than his leading man and was attempting the difficult task of combined writer-director duties for the first time. Considering Hurt's demanding attitude that people be completely knowledgeable about their duties and respect him if he was to respect them, Kasdan was being tested strenuously. That he not only survived the test but emerged as a close friend to Hurt, and the director of his next film, proved that the young West Virginian, who grew up poor and in love with the movies, conducted his business completely in control.

"Larry Kasdan takes a great joy in passing on ideas," said Hurt. "I think that's one mark of great directors. Directors are like a Port Authority of ideas. Ideas are like buses. You know, they come and they park, and the people go and get another bus and they go someplace. That would be the magic of being a director. That would be the joy of it."

Larry Kasdan's fascination with the bright lights of show business comes from the same landscape that nurtured many of America's greatest country and western singers. He grew up in Appalachia, where his family's poverty was no more or less pronounced than that of their neighbors. Kasdan later remembered, "The fact that the most satisfying moments at that time were in a dark theater says something about my childhood." While his future star, William Hurt, was living wonderful and exotic adventures, Kasdan was experiencing them secondhand, and developing the desire to create his own.

While studying writing and English literature at the University of Michigan in Ann Arbor, Kasdan had his first opportunity to see major foreign films, as well as the work of America's formative directors, such as John Ford and Howard Hawks. Aware that writers might also direct, Kasdan plunged himself into the world of cinema with that lofty goal in mind. He began writing scripts in 1968, though almost a decade would elapse before he made his first sale. He persisted, sometimes going through incredible disappointments. One script he wrote, which at least got him an agent, was submitted to several studios for a total of sixty-seven times over the course of two years, but nothing came of it.

Shuttling around between Los Angeles and Detroit, where he got a master's in English and education, Kasdan made his living writing advertising copy, until he came up with *Continental Divide* during a lunch hour and it attracted the attention of four studios, including Steven Spielberg's. Through Spielberg, who made that moderately successful film with John Belushi and Blair Brown (shortly before she filmed *Altered States*), Kasdan met George Lucas. As these true Hollywood romances go, Kasdan was offered the opportunity to write *Raiders of the Lost Ark,* then took over when the original writer of *The Empire Strikes Back* unexpectedly passed away.

All of a sudden, Larry Kasdan was the hottest ticket in town. The community that had made him sweat reversed itself and flooded him with offers. Instead, Kasdan realized that he was in an ideal situation to ask for writing and directing responsibilities on his next project, a movie that owed its sensibility to the great era of detective *film noir*—*Body Heat.*

Kasdan recalled, "It really started with my feeling about my friends and contemporaries—that we were a generation who had been given a great deal, who believed that the world was ours and that what we wanted to do was what we *would* do. And then we came out and discovered it wasn't true: we had to take work we didn't believe in, very much like other generations did. The reaction to that was a sort of searching around for a quick score, a way to get to it without any pain.

"I decided to insert all that in a melodramatic setting. I was very attracted to *film noir.* I thought there was an analogous moral situation there: when men came back from World War Two, America had lost its innocence, and surely *they* had. Women, and society, had changed radically, and men were very uncertain about what women represented and what new power they had taken on in men's absence. Our world, too, had changed, and we didn't expect it.

"The other reason is that I miss language in film dialogue. *Noir* was rich in it—the dialogue crackles, it has bite. It's heightened, not naturalistic. I wanted to see a movie like that."

As if in contrast to the massive blockbusters and jerky teenage films that accounted for the biggest percentage of their budgets, Hollywood's studios seemed ready to permit an indulgence in tight, dark movies—perhaps suspecting that at least some of its audience would accept more nebulous values than the good guys always triumphing—films that pointed to the darker side of reality. In recent years, this return to genre had worked very well in *Chinatown;* not that well in a remake of one of the original *films noir, The Postman Always Rings Twice*—both, interestingly, starring that paragon of warped reality, Jack Nicholson. It doesn't seem at all strange for William Hurt to have darkened his light blond hair and grown a thin, unpleasant mustache for his part in *Body Heat.* He must have understood that there had to be something subdued and slightly oily about a *film noir* archetype. "There isn't a single admirable character in it," explained Larry Kasdan, "although there should be a lot of sympathetic ones."

Well, that remains a matter of debate. *Body Heat* meant to stalk its audiences, as a screen full of rapacious human animals kept watch over one another, each character looking for a weakness in his or her fellows that might be exploited. Set in summertime, in the mythical town of Miranda Beach, Florida, *Body Heat* offers us one Ned Racine, a lawyer of mixed competence and few virtues. He appears to take little pride in his work, acknowledging screw-ups with an air of resignation, more concerned with ensuring that his sexual needs are regularly satisfied.

On a steamy night, strolling the boardwalk, Racine becomes acquainted with a wise-mouthed, tightly built, very hot number named Matty Walker. "Some day your dick is going to lead you into a very big hassle," Racine's buddy Peter Lowenstein prophetically warns him. But Matty is the kind of woman Racine can't resist—he is drawn to her perhaps as much by the danger of sleeping with a married woman as by her own passion. When, with Matty's encouragement, Ned feels compelled to kill her husband, his path seems inexorably ordained, and it can lead to nothing good.

Racine's apparently fatalistic attitude towards his own life causes him to make enough mistakes to arouse suspicion. He eventually realizes that he has been entrapped and outflanked, but carries through with Matty's plan regardless. Little bits and pieces of evidence start to mount up against the lovers, who are now so entangled in their fevered lovemaking that nothing else seems to matter as much. Racine is duped into a legal miscalculation that gradually throws the glare of attention upon him. Still he does not deviate, even after he is laid low, unable to check his admiration for someone possessed of even less morality than he. *Body Heat* is a cautionary tale with continuing impact for anyone who's ever found themselves drifing through life and yearning for an all-consuming flame to inspire a new sense of purpose, even if that purpose turns out to be their undoing. It's a tale told by unlucky survivors of blasted relationships everywhere.

The viper in question, Matty Walker, had to be a dazzler. She needed to be a woman with "a body you shouldn't be allowed to go out in," as Ned Racine said with breathy admiration, but with palpable intelligence as well. This woman had to be an authentic night crawler, who operated best in moist, dark places. "You're not too smart," she would say in one of her opening remarks to Ned Racine. "I like that in a man." Her name was Kathleen Turner, making a feature film debut as explosively as William Hurt had done just a year earlier.

The sultry, delectable Turner had a grand total of one Off-Off-Broadway role and a part on a daytime soap opera before she successfully auditioned as Matty Walker. But her impact was immediate. Often compared to Lauren Bacall for her looks and Greta Garbo for her unfathomable air of mystery, Turner descended upon Hollywood like a bombshell. "Kathleen doesn't fit into a niche with anybody," enthused Larry Kasdan. "She's very beautiful, with an absolutely magnificent vocal quality. A very strong, wonderfully talented actress. I think she's going to fill a spot in our female stars category that's sorely in need of filling," he quite accurately predicted back in 1981. Turner, of course, has gone on to score in other films that exploited her striking face and figure, most notably *Crimes of Passion,* as well as big-budget adventure movies, including *Romancing the Stone,* and, most recently, the delightful time-warped comedy, *Peggy Sue Got Married.*

In creating Matty, Kasdan wanted to portray a somewhat wicked woman, but also a strong one, one who could stand up to Ned Racine and beat him at his own game. He revealed, "My experience with women is that they're strong, intelligent, resourceful and tough—and those are the characters that always interested me. Matty is very much like Ned. It just happens that she's a little better off. What they want is very similar, and even though he imagines himself to be the effective, competent one, she is really the more conscientious and relentless. . . . She represents a lot of things to him and they're very closely tied with basic American drives, images of success."

Turner's recollections of Matty are more directed to the way *Body Heat*'s viewers remember her: "The classic bitch. And worse, she got away with it! She wasn't punished! She had such a strong impact that people had a hard time remembering that I was *not* Matty Walker," Turner told *Playboy* interviewer David Sheff. "For a long time, men had a kind of chip on the shoulder, like, 'You aren't going to put anything over on me, honey.'"

As technicians in Los Angeles skillfully reproduced the glaring days and misty, dank nights of the South Florida coast, Kasdan and his principal players conquered their early concerns about the film, some of which were fairly deep-seated—particularly when it came to matters of sex. "I'm embarrassed about my body," William Hurt admitted. "I don't bare my body easily. But in *Body Heat*, I finally realized that we are always naked—clothed or unclothed," he concluded in typical philosophical style.

Turner explained in somewhat more practical terms how she and Hurt, meeting each other and working together for the first time, learned to deal with the kind of intimate scenes that made *Body Heat* fully deserve its R rating. "Larry and Bill and I would block out the moves in advance and know what we were going to do in front of the camera, so we would be comfortable with it. And the three of us became close throughout the work.

"But you have to get over this hump—at some point, you have to kiss the other person and hug the other person. It was easier to get over that when we were alone than with the crew standing there. So we just walked through the scenes, not performing the actions, not acting them out, but exploring them. Then, when the tension got real heavy, we'd have races up and down the lawn, stuff like that."

In fact, the major problem Hurt seemed to experience came as the result of his working too hard. Three months of eighty-hour weeks gave rise to a fever and daily bouts of nausea. The actor had to buy a heavy-duty parka and wear it—this in Southern California—just to keep the chills at bay. Yet as soon as the film was done and the wrap party over, Hurt flew back to New York and, without a break, started rehearsals for his next Circle Repertory play.

William Hurt's professionalism, and what some might judge his stubborness until proven wrong, helped to make *Body Heat* a successful directorial debut, in Kasdan's opinion. He was, surprisingly, somewhat fearful of actors, despite the support he had already received as a scriptwriter. He explained, "I was worried I wouldn't have the vocabulary that would mean anything to them. I immediately discovered that each actor had his own vocabulary and that I had to deal with each of them differently.

"Hurt is an astounding talent and working with him was a delight and an education, because he constantly challenges you to be better and reexamine your ideas. He's very serious—and he challenges everyone on the set to be that way too. He has a wonderful sense of humor, though, and it was a very happy set.

"But filmmaking . . . is antithetical to the privacy and space an actor needs. What Bill was great about was reminding me of the need for that seriousness. . . . Bill is aggressive about staking out his right—and he was a wonderful influence on everyone. It was clear there was a passion at work."

Admittedly, William Hurt was passionate. So was Kathleen Turner. And so, in his dedication to an ideal and a genre, was Lawrence Kasdan. However, the passions of the critics, following the premiere of *Body Heat* in August, 1981, were sharply divided. Depending upon whether or not one was willing to accept the movie as a modern interpretation of classic *film noir* or insisted that it was simply a tired, clichéd rendering of a decades-old genre, Kasdan was a visionary—or a fake. Prestigious publications lined up to hail or condemn the enterprise.

New York magazine's David Denby not only disliked the

film, but was downright cruel in his assessment of Kathleen Turner, commenting, "there's no soul, no actress there. She's sultry yet humorless, an embarrassing combination, and she moans everything—even the most straightforward expository lines." In the opinion of Denby, the actress even drowned her leading man. "Hurt can't play with Kathleen Turner, and he becomes oddly recessive and almost weak-spirited." Yet the voice that Denby labeled "an aroused foghorn," *Time* reviewer Richard Corliss enjoyed as "a sultry baritone," to go with Turner's "come-hither looks." And what Denby slammed as "a self-conscious imitation of those deliciously paranoid forties pictures," Corliss raved about. "*Body Heat* has more narrative drive, character congestion, and sense of place than any original screenplay since *Chinatown,*" he wrote. "Yet it leaves room for some splendid young actors to breathe, to collaborate in creating the film's texture."

Even at *The New York Times,* reviewers begged to differ with one another. Covering the film at its opening, Janet Maslin criticized Kasdan's heavy reliance "upon old movie motives," rendering the story line implausible for her. "They don't make movies like that anymore," she quipped, "but oh, how they try." On the other hand, Sunday *Times* columnist Vincent Canby examined the film several months later, after the dust (and the heat and the misty night) had cleared, and pronounced it "one of the year's most elegant surprises. I can't remember a film debut to equal it, that is, when a director has made a first film as fully and intelligently realized as *Body Heat.* With one giant leap, Mr. Kasdan has made the big time."

Moderately successful when it was first released, *Body*

Heat has become a perennial favorite of the home video market. And perhaps that's as it should be; the film exudes such overwhelming, straight-to-the-loins sexual appetites that it seems better suited to delectation in the intimacy of one's own boudoir.

One thing was certain—*Body Heat* had put William Hurt on the map, and as a major landmark. Writers felt compelled to predict that his sexual appeal demanded he be voted the next superstar. (Comparisons to Robert Redford, another sexy Wasp, were most abundant.) However, the more acute comments dealt with Hurt's impressive emotional range. "He seems thoughtful, wry and funny, yet he has a comfortable physical presence, too, and a friendliness that's uncomplicatedly disarming," said Maslin. Corliss praised his "economy of gesture. He acts with his eyes and his voice; under pressure, his head snaps into a stare that means to burn into the viewer's skull, and his voice exhales intellectual urgency, as if a dangerous possibility had just slapped him on the back. He seems at once charmingly reasonable and wildly driven—a watcher and a leader." William Hurt was a star, but a star on his own mercurial terms.

6

The Big Chill

EVERYTHING YOU ALWAYS WANTED TO KNOW ABOUT BOOMERS

Perhaps it was logical for people to assume that William Hurt would do the "right things" to preserve his recently acquired star billing. In other words, that he would pursue other, splashier leading roles, be seen in at least some of the right places, and maybe unbend sufficiently to appear somewhat accessible. Those who held such presumptions were quite mistaken, on all counts. Always reluctant to make comments, apart from what his work expressed, Hurt did his rare yearly quotient of interviews "to understand the process," and definitely not to reveal. His life remained private, with a country retreat in New Hampshire, his choice of location, a solid eleven-hour drive from New York City and spiritual light-years away from Los Angeles.

And, most surprisingly, with three attention-getting leading roles under his belt, Hurt then abandoned the film world for close to a year to appear in a television drama and act Shakespeare in the New York Central Park summer festival. Both were roles that downplayed the sexual heat that riveted critics and viewers of his films, a projection the actor never intended to outshine his innate talent and painstakingly learned craft.

Hurt once admitted, "If I wear glasses and my hair's messed up and I'm in old clothes, nobody notices me. I'm so

. . . I hate to say, normal. I'm a basic, man-next-door type. I'm not some big, charismatic star type, so maybe that's why I'll never be Burt Reynolds. I'm not glamorous. My home life is ordinary and I like it private. I also try to keep a distance between myself and L.A."

He concluded, "I don't like being recognized, and I'm not."

What Hurt construed as private, other people started to acknowledge as unpredictable. Asked the same question twice, on one occasion he might respond in clear, direct prose, but with the next variation, Hurt might just as easily commence a philosophical onslaught that would leave his listener completely baffled. An incident that attested to his eccentricity occurred when the actor was giving a tribute to Burt Lancaster at the New York Film Critics Awards. As Hurt turned a simple testimonial into a torrent of verbiage, the guest of honor, like everyone else, was completely in the dark as to what exactly he was going on about. On another occasion, Hurt lambasted a reporter for being late for an interview appointment with him and several other members of the *Big Chill* cast. As the scene was depicted, Hurt remained moody throughout the evening, alternating between incisive, questing remarks, incomprehensible treatises, and clear-cut replies. The interview concluded abruptly when the journalist praised Hurt's acting, to which he responded, "Fuck you."

Clearly, William Hurt was not about to fulfill anyone else's expectations of what a leading man–movie star ought to say and do. His only responsibilities were to himself and the people he worked with on each project, helping them make the film or play the best it could be. He harbored no false illusions about the nature of the medium, or the glamor mystique that perpetuated itself both within the industry and outside it. For Hurt, the essence of communication rested with the honest dialogue of the actors, not the technique or the hardware.

"The camera is just a big black box," he said. "It's plastic and metal. It doesn't transform anything. We let it. There is nothing mysterious about it. The mystery had existed for a long time, long before the camera—with people getting together and talking about things they didn't understand. It's people that make it happen. If the camera becomes strong, all human input is nullified—the camera becomes an element of intimidation. You could supposedly force someone to do a brilliant piece of work, but if you didn't ask the person for his best motives, he wouldn't come up with his best work, no matter what."

When, late in 1982, Hurt accepted his fourth film role, it was not as the leading man. Or rather, it was as one of seven leading men and women in the ensemble movie, *The Big Chill.* Obviously, Hurt relished doing ensemble work, and to date that film remains the closest he has come to fulfilling the theatrical ideal he takes as the norm in his stage work. Having enormously enjoyed working with Larry Kasdan on *Body Heat,* Hurt relished the experience of again teaming up with the visionary, if young director, who once more had come up with a concept that reflected directly upon his own experiences and yearnings.

The sixties remain the most self-reflective decade of modern American history, thanks in large part to the aging of the young people who made it twist and shout. The sixties teenagers and young adults are today's yuppies and early middle-agers, filled with lots of heady recollections and regretfully aware of the very different times they now live in. By sheer force of numbers (eighty million born between the post–World War Two era and the mid-sixties), this "baby boom" generation forced things to happen, forced people to sit up and take notice. As they grow older, they cannot escape the equally profound awareness of how much both society and themselves have changed and how, if in any way, they remain the same.

They were born into a time of affluence and optimism, although their parents had survived a catastrophic depression and one, if not two, world wars. The baby boomers entered the world along with the atomic bomb, the long-playing record, and the initial marketing of television sets. Their parents, using minimal down payments and easy-to-handle mortgages courtesy of the GI bills, populated former farmland or wilderness country that was being transformed into suburbs. In retrospect, this determination to be the best, do the best, and have the best practically guaranteed that the resulting generation of young people would be raised with high expectations indeed, if not with a feeling of invincibility.

At the same time as this mass of youth was being educated, their parents and their country were suffused with the values of conformity. Differences of belief had been resolved by the recent world war; therefore, to remain cohesive, Americans wanted to look, act, and think alike. Of course, sometimes, as in the reign of Senator Joseph McCarthy and his Communist conspiracy headhunters, it went a little too far, but for the most part Americans were glad to wear their gray flannel suits and tend their detached aluminum-sided homes with their white picket fences. They taught their children the glorious three-hundred-year history of America's manifest destiny (brushing over such unfortunate incidents as black slavery and the extermination of the Indians). Children believed that other, non-American ways of living were wrong as fervently as they believed that hiding under the school desk would save them in an atomic attack.

There were signs, however, that this smooth surface was only a veneer. During the fifties, a landmark civil rights case came before the Supreme Court, which ordered school desegregation, a ruling that was sometimes only complied with after violent resistance had ensued. With the unexpected and disarming popularity of rock and roll, crafty marketers sensed that "teenagers"—and their millions of disposable allowance dollars—constituted a potentially lucrative target audience, completely apart from their parents. As much as the teens themselves did, those who created products just for them began to drive a wedge between the generations.

But it was during the sixties that the vision of an omnipotent America came to a crashing end for many of its citizens. The 1963 assassination of President John F. Kennedy announced that America was not invulnerable to internal terrorism. The escalation of combat in Vietnam led many to question the wisdom of interfering in another nation's civil conflict at the cost of thousands of lives. Simultaneously, groups that had felt the American dream pass them by began to demand their rights; where were the equal opportunities for Blacks, Hispanics, students, women, and gay people? The ideal vision of America perpetrated in the "silent generation" fifties didn't hold up under the challenges of the sixties. Whether by fighting the system politically or by more radical means, or by dropping out of it with hallucinogenic drugs or communal living arrangements, sixties youth demanded an America in which the ideal and the reality really were one.

This goal, unfortunately, would never be attained. Though many reforms were achieved by women and minority groups, and the war in Vietnam did end after a decade, as they matured, the sixties youth found themselves forced to make compromises. Macrobiotic diets, communes, and carpentry gave way, in most cases, to nouvelle cuisine, marriage or long-term partnerships, and MBAs. While seeing themselves as liberal on social issues, much of the sixties generation were willingly pulled to the right, politically and economically, along with the less self-questioning generation that followed them. The term *young urban professional,* or "yuppie," was coined to replace the hippie of that other era.

But, unwilling to completely forget the people they once had been, the baby boomers fell into conflict with themselves. Had they totally abandoned their ideals? If not, how much had compromise changed them and what part of themselves was still pure? With these questions lurking underneath the unfurrowed brow of many a boomer's head as he pounded down the jogging track, along came fellow boomer Lawrence Kasdan to bring that hidden agenda to light in *The Big Chill.*

Said Kasdan, "*The Big Chill* deals with members of my generation who have also discovered that not everything they wanted is possible, that not every ideal they believed in has stayed in the forefront of their intentions. *The Big Chill* is about a cooling process that takes place for every generation when they move from the outward-directed, more idealistic concerns of their youth to a kind of self-absorption, a self-interest which places their personal desires above those of the society or even an ideal."

While dealing with a cast of characters who came to consciousness during the sixties and using actors who were in their teens during that time, Kasdan intended that the film express this conflict in a way that other generations might relate to.

"To me the basic theme of *The Big Chill* is the reconstruction of hope," said William Hurt. "I don't think we're particularly unusual as a generation. I think everybody's probably been through it in some way or another." Yet the actor, as if in recognition of how personalizing the experience was for him, dubbed it "the best home movie ever made.

"If you do something simply and from the heart, something that you feel applies specifically to your life, you reach the widest possible audience. The audience will then experience what you feel. I call that bit of logic the 'great unified theorem of the lowest common denominator,'" he concluded in typical Hurt philosophical style.

So inwardly focused was the movie that it's debatable whether it contains a story line or simply came to its conclusions from a series of interdependent vignettes. Seven college friends—four men and three women—have come together to be at the funeral of their old chum Alex, a brilliant yet apparently unresolved individual who has killed himself. They spend the following weekend together in the rambling, painstakingly homey abode of a running-shoe tycoon and his wife, a doctor. The five other personalities are a lawyer who wants a baby, the star of an action-adventure

TV series who can't handle emotional commitment, a well-off married woman who wants a change, a *People* magazine reporter who's disgusted with his work, and a Vietnam veteran, emasculated in battle, who deals drugs as his way of kicking back at the system. There's also Alex's girlfriend, so much younger than everyone else that she cannot comprehend the twists and turns they put themselves through, or the disappointments of their lives, which plague them.

"All these people, though they're in their thirties, still think of themselves as kids," says Larry Kasdan. "I didn't want the film to lose sight of one central theme, the need for meaningful, satisfying work. I think people of my generation had high expectations they would get the sort of work they wanted and that may turn out to be one of the few, real traits which distinguished people who grew up in the sixties from their parents, or even their successors. A lot of people in my parents' generation had no expectations that they'd be happy in their work. My generation thought we'd be happy in everything."

Well, over the course of the weekend, a lot of those seemingly fulfilled expectations are proven to be fraught with pockets of discontent. Alliances shift and twitch as old yearnings and deep-seated resentments bubble up from twenty-year-old burial mounds to cast new scars. It soon becomes obvious that no one's life has turned out exactly the way he or she always believed it would. And this "chilling" awareness would always stay with them. The title of the film was quite deliberate, says its creator, who invested it with two meanings.

"These people think of themselves as kids. These are people who have an endless belief in their own possibilities, and suddenly they see that for Alex, the possibilities are over." And it is with growing awareness, continued the director, that one could never assume one's ideals would stay untouched forever. "It's this feeling I would get when I was talking to someone with whom I felt I shared a lot of sympathy. Suddenly they would say something—or I would say it—that was so out of bounds or so cold or so cynical that a chill would pass over me. It's this feeling of being totally reversed."

Larry Kasdan wholeheartedly believed in *The Big Chill* and, with his very ambitious track record, felt that he would have no trouble generating studio interest. However, it didn't turn out that way. Hollywood was filled with up-and-coming studio executives, who if they intended to rise to the top, gamely sacrificed whatever ideals they might have had to the necessity of playing the system's game. Patently uncomfortable with a rather introspective film—with eight co-stars, without a defined romance or lots of sex, sans action, violence, or splashy special effects—that poked dangerously close to where their own self-doubts were buried, they rejected the film. Kasdan went through similar treatment at a total of fifteen companies before Carson Productions came up with the necessary financing.

A splended group of actors was selected to make up this ensemble group—all in their thirties except for twenty-three-year-old Meg Tilly, who portrayed Alex's girlfriend, Chloe. Kevin Kline and Glenn Close were the married couple, Mary Kay Place the lawyer and would-be mother, Jeff Goldblum the magazine writer, Tom Berenger the TV star, Jobeth Williams the unhappily married lady, and, no surprise here, William Hurt as Nick, the impotent and bitterly angry drug dealer. (This time, Hurt could be viewed as a sex symbol only in terms of what might have been. That didn't stop the women—on-screen and off—from finding him attractive.)

Rehearsals were held both in Los Angeles and the town of Beaufort, South Carolina, where Kasdan located the statuesque edifice that served as Harold and Sarah's home. The intensive preparation period, lasting a month, allowed the actors ample time to become comfortable with one another, at times blurring the distinctions between the players and their roles. Hurt was caught somewhat off guard by Kasdan's plan. "Attacking the notion of the separation between yourself and your work is extremely subtle and disturbing, and can be very unsettling," he admitted.

"An actor's work is hard enough," Kasdan commented. "No matter how much preparation, no matter how much background you give them about the text, one way you can really help is by giving them more time to get familiar with the other performers. On a movie about friends you want the actors to have some of the intimacy that long friendships would create."

The director's instincts turned out to be right on target. As weeks passed, the eight individual actors, some of whom had known one another but others who had not, began to form their own friendships. Kevin Kline and Jeff Goldblum shared a rented house, where they would often entertain their colleagues over dinner after work. They also exchanged confidences, Hurt recalled, about their lives during the sixties. Experiences ranged from Hurt's, who felt "fear and shame and independence" about the era, since he had never joined any movements or large protests, to Kline's, who acted in an antiwar play in college, to Jobeth Williams's, the only one in the group who had been an active protester. "I was teargassed in Washington," she revealed. "Filming *Big Chill* was like a time warp for me." In fact, Kasdan had shot a flashback sequence showing the characters as they had been during the sixties, but cut it out because he felt that he couldn't authentically reproduce the decade. Ironically, some critics later wrote that a problem with the movie lay with exactly that omission—one had little sense of who these characters had been, as compared to what they had become.

"We talked about whether you have indeed lived up to the promises you made to yourself in your youth," Hurt explained. "A great many of us who thought we were going to save the world went underground. We saw that our magnificent dreams were not going to come true. A lot of us became extremely quiet, extremely shy. [One senses that the actor is doing a bit of self-reflection here.] But the dreams are still there. They're just older and wiser, a lot more modest, a lot more shy."

Kasdan's final trick before filming began came in the form of a marathon improvisation. Each actor stayed in character for over five hours, during which time the director left them alone. What began as a decision to cook a meal together turned into an experience that exhausted the group but ultimately united them.

"They remained in character without any authority figure," said Kasdan, "without any director to tell them if they were behaving or reacting in the correct way, according to the writer's or director's ideas. They had to live in those characters' skins and instantly deal with input from each other character. . . . [It] happened at a crucial, crystalizing moment, and it turned eight individual actors into an ensemble."

When *The Big Chill* premiered in September, 1983, after opening at the New York Film Festival, it drew almost predictably mixed reactions. Critics proved as susceptible to the mystique of the sixties as did viewers, and shaded their responses according to their own precepts of how that era's survivors had measured up. Some, like David Denby, reviewer for *New York* magazine (a stronghold of yuppie ideals), openly rejected its foundation. He wrote, "*The Big Chill* may be nostalgic for the late sixties, but it's been shrewdly designed for the Reagan eighties. . . . For Kasdan, the sixties seems to be a time when people were nice to one another . . . A few puffs of pot, a communal weekend, a friendly gesture of dubious sanity—as an epitaph for a generation, it's not much, is it? The characters in *The Big Chill* are first patted on the back for having had ideals and then teased for so easily giving them up. The movie is doubly patronizing and it displays the infuriating, dumb cynicism of people who know nothing of life outside show business."

Quite different was the reaction of *Time* critic Richard Corliss, who felt the film touched a universal chord and related to other generations besides the one that acted in it. He opined, "One of the nice things about this funny and ferociously smart movie is that it is not only about the sixties. Instead, it works from several assumptions about those times to create an impromptu dormitory of likeable individuals who know each other well enough to can the sloganeering. Much more is exposed by the way people walk and sit, by the not quite facetious insult, by the silent, shared memory. This is a movie about getting through a weekend without being bored or driven to tears, about bull sessions that become psychodramas, about making do and making love and making breakfast in the morning." In fact, Corliss went so far as to call *The Big Chill*—in part because of its excellent, call-up-the-nostalgia soundtrack, "the feel-good movie of '83."

Yet even if they faulted the movie, most reviewers had nothing but praise for its accomplished cast. Kasdan had at least achieved his goal of getting the actors to get into their parts as second skins. The now-usual comments about William Hurt's eyes "like restless laser beams" and his "cutting anger"—qualities that had drawn attention in earlier films—were supplemented with new insights about his extraordinarily effective self-discipline.

"Only the power of Hurt's cold-fever performance makes us overlook the heavy-handedness of his symbolic emasculation," stated David Ansen in *Newsweek*. When David Denby first encountered Hurt's embittered war veteran, he found himself on unsteady ground. "This self-conscious actor puts quotation marks around everything he says, and I couldn't tell right away if he was giving a pretentious performance or effectively playing a pretentious man." Despite Denby's mistrust, he then had to concede, "Hurt may have become too private and eccentric to play well with anyone else, but when he shows us the vulnerable side of this arrogant hipster, we realize that he knows exactly what he's doing." And *People* magazine's reviewer didn't mince words, defining William Hurt as "first-rate."

In retrospect, *The Big Chill* left a legacy that Larry Kasdan may not have intended as his desired result. It gave the stamp of legitimacy to a generation that had, in fact, abandoned a great many of its earlier dreams for a compromise with reality and was now bemoaning that loss of faith—without ever doing anything to correct it. It made the sixties seem somehow quaint—not the angry, turbulent, and challenging times they were—to the generation that succeeded the early baby boomers, those yuppies who acknowledge few ideals and no constraints, except within the marketplace. To that end, in keeping with the current ethic, it obliquely condemned Hurt's drug seller character, while praising Kevin Kline's high-end-market sneaker seller, though both men were giving the public what it wanted. And it offered the sixties as a selling tool, where the soundtrack that recaptured an era might next be used to sell everything from raisins to automobiles. *The Big Chill* was of far greater consequence as a successful ensemble piece than it was as a moral agenda.

"What is so utterly frustrating about *The Big Chill*," said Abbie Hoffman, who, as a major sixties radical personality, should know, "is that it is a lot like meeting a student who got an A in a course, yet somehow managed to miss the point entirely. The movie could just as easily have scored high marks without resorting to such a trite interpretation of the generational aging process, an interpretation not only safe in its triteness but not even entirely true."

7

Gorky Park

WHEN THE TRUTH HURTS

"I accept that everybody's got their styles," William Hurt once said, "but I don't let them inflict it on me. I don't work with shitheads! Even if they're brilliant. If I start smelling this stuff, I crawl into my hole.

"Ingmar Bergman once said, 'If you feel anxiety as an artist, it's your duty to express it.' While the reality as it takes place on the set is not the only reality present, it's still a very important one. If I feel anger, I can't hide from it. You take it with you."

Hurt, in making *The Big Chill,* had been working in an environment that encouraged total disclosure. Not only was the film itself a sort of psychodrama, focusing on the intimate relationships between old and once close friends, but its ensemble cast had been urged to share all of their feelings, whether warm or angry. For his next movie, Hurt would be operating in a very different milieu. Its environment was as frosty and bare as that of *Big Chill* was leafy and lush. And where *Big Chill* celebrated personalities at their most expansive, this project, *Gorky Park,* prescribed characters who were totally under control, who operated under rules as tight as the Russian state that was their homeland. The tales that came back from *Gorky Park*'s locations in Finland hinted at artistic anxieties being violently unleashed, and they were impossible to ignore. William Hurt, in his fifth movie, was the unyielding focal point of this film. Perhaps it was those correspondingly heavy demands that prompted his undeniably difficult behavior.

Until shortly before *Gorky Park* actually began filming, Hurt wasn't even involved with the movie. A lot was expected from this adaptation of Martin Cruz Smith's best-selling novel. The book was a runaway smash in the early eighties, a well-plotted, intricately researched thriller that elevated Smith to the pantheon of great intrigue writers such as Robert Ludlum, John le Carré, and Frederick Forsyth. Smith dealt with a tantalizing subject—a hero who was a Soviet policeman on the trail of an unknown murderer. In a genre where all Russians tended, from necessity and precedent, to be bad guys on the wrong side of truth and justice, Smith's Arkady Renko was as honorable as any sleuth of the Western world. Millions of readers willingly dropped their preconceptions about this one Russian and cheered him on as he resisted the true evils inside his society to unmask the killer. In the course of the chase, Smith delivered an impressive fund of knowledge about Soviet culture, all the way from high-level bureaucratic perks to the small maneuverings of its citizens attempting to get some tidbit of the action, living as they did in a climate of scarcity.

When Arkady Renko, chief investigator of the Militia (somewhat akin to a U.S. city's police department), discovers the mutilated bodies of two men and one woman in the snows of Gorky Park, he suspects that his rivals, the far more powerful KGB, were involved. The bodies have no fingertips or faces; all Renko can determine is their sex.

Having already crossed the KGB once and been beaten

for it, Renko is surprised that the clandestine bureau seems willing to give him a free hand with his investigation. But he is soon preoccupied with a beautiful dissident girl named Irina, whose ice skates were found on the murdered girl's body. Irina, obsessed with the hope of one day reaching the West and sanctuary, believes that her friends have in fact been ushered to freedom by a wealthy American, Osborne, who, as a trader of sables, practically has carte blanche inside the Soviet Union.

Only after Renko proves to Irina that her friends were indeed butchered is he able to focus on catching the murderer, who, he realizes, is being protected by very high-up sources within the KGB. Renko has an unlikely ally in his quest, a hard-boiled New York cop, Kirwill, whose idealistic younger brother was one of the victims. Eventually, Renko uncovers Osborne's secret plan—that he intends to break Russia's long-standing sable monopoly by smuggling several live animals out of the country.

Renko, learning that Irina has left his country with the hateful Osborne, believes she has double-crossed him, despite their budding love, as well as acted like a traitor. However, she tearfully confides that Osborne has a secret he's kept back even from the KGB officials with whom he had bargained. Ordered to intercept Osborne in Sweden and make sure that neither the American nor the priceless sables leave that country, Renko must play a dangerous game of wits to keep himself and Irina alive. But even if he survives this deadly intrigue, the stalwart investigator faces an equally rigorous test of the heart—will he and Irina ever be able to live together in happiness and freedom?

Gorky Park seemed like an ideal choice for an East-West

novel to be transferred to the screen. Although a certain amount of bureaucratic complexity was described, it was not so convoluted as to confound the viewer. There was engrossing romance between Renko and Irina; a surprise bad guy in the form of the American entrepreneur, Osborne; and a partnership born of opposition but grown into respect and brotherhood between the Russian policeman and his American counterpart.

Careful planning went into the casting of the movie: Lee Marvin accepted the role of Osborne, Brian Dennehy was to play the veteran cop, Kirwill, and the young Polish actress Joanna Pacula was tapped for the part of Irina. At first, Dustin Hoffman was said to be interested in playing Arkady Renko, and reports appeared saying that he had even begun to learn Russian. However, by the fall of 1982, Hoffman was out and William Hurt had secured the pivotal part. The main reason was said to be financial: Hoffman held out for almost five million dollars, while Hurt agreed to a much more reasonable million-dollar price tag. And with costs that eventually topped thirteen million dollars, the producers as well as director Michael Apted felt confident that Hurt would be the kind of Renko they envisioned. (Don't cry for Dustin's lost opportunity; he went on to star in the Oscar-winning comedy *Tootsie.*)

"One of the major decisions I had to make on *Gorky Park* was how to play the voices," Apted explained in an interview. "I decided to have English actors with English accents play the Russians, which is why the two Americans in the film could be played by Americans. Since everybody in the film speaks Russian, we could substitute English." In this respect, Hurt fit the bill perfectly. Because he had spent close to a year studying in Britain, he was able to approximate a fairly seamless English accent.

"Hurt really looks Slavic," the director pointed out. "We dyed his hair and combed it backwards. He's a distinguished actor and I was very impressed by the range of what he's done, by his willingness to give new things a crack. . . . He's open and vulnerable and loves to rehearse and figure things out. He's very hard-working and collaborative, very interested in other actors, very generous. And also," Apted said delicately, "meticulous and difficult. . . ." (As it happened, Hurt began work on his part using a Slavic accent until Apted tactfully suggested that they ought to try something else.)

Since directing his first film in 1972, British director Michael Apted had proved adaptable to both low-cost projects and ambitious works. His previous credits included the satiric rock musical comedy, *Stardust*, the critically acclaimed adaptation of country music star Loretta Lynn's autobiography, *Coal Miner's Daugher*, which starred Sissy Spacek, and John Belushi's unsuccessful attempt to carry a romantic lead, *Continental Divide* (which also starred Blair Brown, fresh from her role opposite William Hurt in *Altered States.*) Described by critic Dan Yakir as "a brilliant craftsman," Apted remained an innovative director working within the Hollywood mainstream since the mid-seventies. His films tended to feature unexpected, often quirky pairings, such as Belushi and Brown, and to him, authenticity of locations was worth any amount of difficulty, if the results rang true.

"I felt the book by Martin Cruz Smith was a fresh territory," he said. "It offered me the opportunity to create a gallery of Russian characters that haven't been seen on the screen before. It's a familiar story set against an alien background, but this background and the choice of characters produce an end result that is original. . . . If I succeeded in making it accessible, in making the thriller work, then people could take something from the background as well."

To achieve that intention, the producers of *Gorky Park*, Gene Kirkwood and Howard W. Koch, Jr., began the painstaking task of securing the most accurate setting for its complex plot. The best place, of course, would have been inside the Soviet Union. Koch and Kirkwood actually went to Moscow as tourists, hoping to get official cooperation. It was no surprise, though, that as soon as the powers that be learned that the film in question was to be *Gorky Park*, with its highly political critique of the men at the top, the Americans wore out their welcome and were turned down flat.

A stickler for reality in his work, Michael Apted was determined to compensate for having to shift *Gorky Park* to Helsinki, Finland, the large Western city nearest the Soviet border that approximated the physical landscape and weather conditions of Moscow. Apted was relentless in his research. He, too, went to Moscow as a tourist, picking up as much of the people's daily routine as an outsider was permitted to note. Back in America, the filmmakers interviewed Russian émigrés, devoured countless volumes about the country, and viewed dozens of Soviet films and television shows.

Apted obtained some invaluable source material when production designer Paul Sylbert also visited Russia on a tourist's visa. After allowing an Intourist guide to supervise him for a couple of days, Sylbert went out on his own, photographing and drawing anything he felt was distinctively

Russian. No detail, no matter how small, escaped his practiced eye. For instance, anyone who was going to Russia was ordered to bring back the Soviet cigarettes that Renko smoked throughout the film. "At first Hurt hated them, but he smoked them the whole way through like a trooper," one executive recalled.

Sylbert even shot off some film of Militia headquarters until he realized that someone was watching him. Fortunately, he managed a getaway in a taxi. He brought back over twenty rolls of film and several sketchbooks.

However, when costume designer Richard Bruno, faced with the task of devising several thousand pieces of Russian-type apparel, spent a week in Moscow, he did get caught photographing military officers. His film was confiscated and the unlucky Bruno was locked in his room for two days. "I was happy to get out of there, even empty-handed," he said with understandable relief.

In the end, Apted and the producers, working in Helsinki, achieved an admirable recreation of Soviet life. Everything from the design of apartments to clothing for two thousand extras was matched by the tireless crew, who strived for authenticity in the film's close to one hundred sets. "I think *Gorky Park* has a great contrast; it shows that there is wealth, breeding, and culture on one side and a sort of poverty on the other side," Michael Apted observed. "I think they are two valid sides of Russia and I wanted to show them both. I didn't want to miss the culture of Russian society. It was difficult to find opportunities but I managed to put a string quartet into the film as well as Russian music, from folk songs to Tchaikovsky. I wanted to pay deference to what is admirable in Russian society."

The director insisted that, despite the Soviets' noncooperation with his crew, which forced them to shoot outside Russia, he wasn't interested in creating a piece of propaganda. Throughout the film, as in the book, Arkady Renko is shown to be a man who loves his country, although he is maddened by and determined to avenge the corruption he perceives penetrating some of its highest bastions. "In a way," said Apted, "the warmest relationship in the film is between Arkady and Kirwill; an American cop who is looking for his lost brother and a Russian cop who tracks him down discover that they have the same enemy, that they are on the same side. I wanted to avoid the clichés of the wisecracking American cop—and casting Hurt certainly helped me in that: he's not a wisecracking kind of actor.

"I'm not making a political film," the director continued. "I tried to make the characters as compassionate as possible, but still I had a story to tell. There have to be villains, there have to be heroes. I was hired to make a best-selling novel into a film, and the story is about corruption in many levels of Russian society—people feathering their nests, people trying to get out, people pulling scams. I have tried to be faithful to the spirit of the book. I can't turn it into a polemic to Russian society or a paean to the Communist system. I can't do that. But, of course, any film about Russia is going to be considered a political film."

Being so close to the Russian border as they set to work in Helsinki, the crew was aware of a conscious Soviet presence, although it was often disguised. They felt certain that several KGB agents followed their every move, and suspected at least a few local people of reporting their activities to the Russians. Fortunately, the interference was more annoying than threatening. It took the form of inconveniences, such as the time they found it unnecessarily difficult to obtain a Russian washing machine because all the normal avenues of trade were suddenly closed off. And, of course, since obtaining Soviet sables to use in the film was out of the question, the filmmakers settled for Finnish look-alikes.

Arriving in Helsinki in January, 1983, to begin rehearsals for *Gorky Park,* Hurt felt artistically stimulated and personally satisfied by the central role of Arkady Renko. This police officer was neither a blood-and-guts, flag-waving good guy nor a taciturn, one-man avenger. He was a complex man up against the unbending rules of an authoritarian society, who must search inside himself for the right things to do. Playing another nonconformist also suited the actor, who repeatedly sought out individuals rather than stereotypes.

"To me, that's artistic integrity," he said of representing a man such as Arkady Renko. "Most people, whatever their nationality or profession, are not flamboyant or larger than life. I'm not that comfortable if asked to play an out-and-out villain or a big hero—neither are real. Life's gray, not black and white.

"I kept thinking about the notion of dignity. I admire stalwart people who don't pretend to comprehend everything around them but have a notion of good and pursue it even though they know they'll get blown away in time, chopped down. They know they have no real power, but they persist in doing what they believe in."

Echoing the thoughts of Michael Apted, Hurt continued, "but criticism of the regime in *Gorky Park* is not at all what it's about. I came to a staggering idea of just what the

Russian price has been in our century, what price that nation has paid. Think of twenty-five to thirty million killed in World War Two alone. You've got to go into the land, put your hands down, and feel the blood. And you think, 'What the hell is going on? What the hell are we making these stupid deductions about each other for? This is ridiculous!'"

It was as one very fervent humanist that Hurt took on the character of Renko, self-contained on the outside but internally, passionate about restoring honor and justice to the country he believed in, which he felt had been damaged by lies. A *Time* magazine reporter visited the set in Helsinki and was unstinting with his praise for the actor, who for this role had been altered pysically as well, his blond hair dyed brown and swept back, instead of falling easily across his high forehead. "He is uncannily good at his job," the correspondent wrote. "As he waits between takes, he is clearly American; as the camera rolls, something too subtle to watch happens to his face—a matter of clouding, of caution—he becomes unquestionably Russian. He is Arkady."

"*Gorky Park* was my first opportunity to go into areas of physical characterization that I wanted to get into," Hurt explained. "Physical differentiation. The mask. Because the mask comes to life. And what do people believe? They believed their imagination. The life that is happening is the life of the imagination. That is in the mind of the actor." Under those conditions, he was able to imagine any circumstance and have it become the reality of that moment. "And we can all take responsibility for it without being ashamed."

Unfortunately, according to various reports that filtered through from the brutal wintertime arena of the Helsinki location, not everything surrounding the *Gorky Park* cast and crew seemed to come from healthy imaginations. It appears that Apted's characterization of Hurt as "difficult" was on the mark in several instances. The actor commented that several of the filmmakers "raped the screenwriter, Dennis Potter," who Hurt had praised as "one of the greatest writers ever." Hurt believed that the filmmakers wanted an action movie, which was diametrically opposed to his reading of the script as "a morality play." Yet Potter described his experiences on the film for one of the London Sunday newspapers and referred to one unnamed actor as having "both paddles out of the water."

Another often told tale concerned Hurt, his co-star, Lee Marvin, and an unnamed British cast member. Hurt praised Marvin, who portrayed the evil Osborne, as supporting his goals for the script, maintaining that the film veteran "acted the hell out of his scenes. He acted better than I did. Instead of trying to beat him, which was of course not my job, I wanted to let this person teach me. . . . And he did—on so many levels you wouldn't believe." However, here again, accounts differ on the real relationship between the two stars. According to one report, the British actor was made to wait in Helsinki's subzero weather, while Hurt sat in a warm trailer for an inordinate amount of time. The actor supposedly confided to Lee Marvin that when Hurt finally came out, he (the Englishman) punched Hurt in the jaw. Marvin's widely publicized reply: "Good, man, you saved me the trouble."

And even Michael Apted, who had praise for Hurt's work in the film—which Hurt returned in kind—was reportedly heard to complain, "I don't understand a word he says." It appears that William Hurt, who demands nothing less than the best from himself, applies his own rigorous standards to those with whom he works. Add to that his propensity for turning the simplest question into a philosophical discourse, and the fact that he is not the most even-tempered man in the world, and it's easy to see that trouble may have been the inevitable result.

Sadly, good intentions, dedicated performances, meticulous attention to detail, and a budget big enough to cover all contingencies did not add up to either critical or commercial success for *Gorky Park.* The story presentation was judged more dull than subtle, and many reviewers found the entire premise unbelievable—perhaps a quibble better taken up with the author of the novel than those who tirelessly and faithfully transferred it to film. Dennis Potter's script was attacked by *Time,* which stated that it "vitiates" the strengths of Smith's novel, *Newsweek,* which charged that the script "fails to generate any compelling human interaction," and *New York,* which merely labeled it "vauge." *Times* critic Janet Maslin was somewhat milder with her reproach, though she, too, cautioned that the film had problems. She wrote, "On the whole, Mr. Apted's approach to the material is archly effective, making for a crisp, intricate thriller, well able to hold an audience's interest. However, viewers unfamiliar with the novel may be better disposed toward the movie than Mr. Smith's readers will be, since the screen version of this detective drama is less effectively atmospheric than the book."

For the first time since he began his film career, William Hurt came in for the brunt of the movie's criticism. Reviewers absolutely hated his English accent, and used it as the departure point for why he failed to move them as Renko. "Hurt's horrendous, with his goofy stilted accent," charged the *Washington Post.* "He talks as though he's swallowed a bathtub." *People* magazine saw Hurt as "receding into the wallpaper, as if he is afraid to project anything."

"For the first time, William Hurt is dead wrong in a role," commented *Newsweek*'s David Ansen. "Putting on an English accent, Hurt gives a cold, stilted performance, like a man buttoned up in an ill-fitting suit." And from Richard Schickel, writing in *Time,* came probably the worst assessment of all: "William Hurt, accent all askew, his spirit turned to molasses by an excess of brooding, plays Arkady as if he were strictly from Chekhov. It is a ludicrous exhibition—possibly the silliest piece of self-consciousness since movies added the Method to their madness."

If it is indeed true that Hurt, as he claims, does not read his reviews, *Gorky Park* was the ideal instance in which he should have followed his own advice.

8

A VERY DIFFERENT MASK

IN THE WEB OF *THE SPIDER WOMAN*

William Hurt was, undeniably, a major film star by now, after five years of making movies. Rarely a week went by in which he was not beseiged with scripts and offers to play parts befitting an actor in the million-dollar-plus salary range. Yet Hurt turned almost all of them down without qualms, and it quickly became clear that no one could predict just what kind of role this introspective yet independent actor might emphathize with. His choices had little in common on the surface, but dig deeper and it was evident that all of Hurt's characters were men who had to make some fundamental discovery, unearth some vital truth, that would forever alter their lives. In sum, the only person who really knew that a part offered the right stimulation to William Hurt was the actor himself.

It didn't matter to him whether the character was intrinsically attractive or if the audience would find him so. Offered the leading man–sex object classification, which was perpetually thrust upon him, Hurt rejected its easy lure. He disguised his looks; in *Gorky Park,* he even disguised his speaking voice. Being true to the character's integrity—after first making sure that such integrity actually existed—was far more important. With Hurt's increasing fame came a corresponding battle to maintain his scruples and preserve the moral fortitude with which he had entered the business.

Hurt recognized the spiritual risks that great wealth and a certain command over the public entailed, and rededicated himself to retaining control over his soul. He once discussed the need to keep one's honor, and though his comments originally referred to honor in general, they very aptly describe his own code of behavior—demanding, but with gratifying inner rewards.

"Poverty and honor walk hand in hand a lot of the time. I know it sounds cruel, but I don't mean it that way at all. But wealth does corrupt and if absolute power corrupts absolutely, then any portion thereof also has a corrupting influence on you. And you have to fight it. I've met some wealthy people who were very good people, but that's not the point. When I worked on a sheep ranch in Australia [he spent a summer there, right after graduating college], it reminded me of the spirit which we might have had in the West in the pioneering days, no matter how many people were killed for it. Sometimes when you have nothing to gain—or when you have everything to gain—you do wonderful things.

"So, what you're trying to do, always, no matter where you are, is create: put yourself in a position where you are contemplating the horizon again without actually getting any closer to it. You just keep going for it." William Hurt had nothing, and everything, to gain when he accepted the role of an imprisoned homosexual window dresser, Luis Molina, in an undercapitalized, obscure film adaptation of an unusually crafted South American novel, *Kiss of the Spider Woman.* And it did prove to be a wonderful thing. At the time he was offered the role, Hurt was still in Finland, working on *Gorky Park.* Raul Julia, the actor who would play

Valentin to Hurt's Molina in the essentially two-character piece, sent him the script. It took Hurt exactly three days to eagerly accept the part that most admirers believe was the most challenging and successfully realized of his career.

Spider Woman could not have described an environment more different from *Gorky Park.* Part of it was physical—a film made for under three million dollars as compared to one costing in the teens. Everything was compressed, made urgent, by the demands of time and budget. But the larger difference had to do with the very nature of the films themselves. Interestingly, both dealt with authoritarian regimes and were adapted from acclaimed novels. However, *Gorky Park* was clearly the product of the Western esthetics of Americans and Englishmen, who felt at ease to imagine and describe the Soviet gloom and suspicions they were depicting. *Spider Woman,* on the other hand, was both written in its novel form and directed by South Americans, who did not always enjoy such freedoms of expression. When author Manuel Puig used the novel to convey the repressive atmosphere of an Argentine prison, his book was refused publication in his own country, although other Spanish-language editions have turned up in Argentine bookstores. Perhaps this chill gave the production its cast of authenticity, which eluded *Gorky Park,* or maybe its international success was simply the rare combination of an engrossing story, appropriate direction, and inspired casting, with all of the participants having no concern besides creating excellence.

"I wanted to explore the basic dynamics of human behavior, and show that sometimes a person becomes trapped in a role when there are possibilities of being many other things," said Manuel Puig, the Argentine-born writer who originally wanted to direct films but instead has published seven novels, which have been widely praised for their experimental form and decisive emotional impact. His love for movies, part of his inner fiber since childhood, remains strong to the present day, and Puig took an active part in assisting screenwriter Leonard Schrader and director Hector Babenco in transferring *Spider Woman* to the screen. Although Puig and Babenco did not know one another before they worked together on the film, their backgrounds reveal two somewhat shy individuals who looked to the creative arts as a refuge from their own insecurities—very similar to William Hurt's rescue from the disappointments of his own childhood through acting.

Manuel Puig grew up in a small town on the Argentine pampas, an unchanging landscape that makes its inhabitants feel like they're in the middle of nowhere. "That place is the absence of landscape," Puig emphasized, and it was not conducive to an atmosphere of spiritual comfort. Puig retreated to the village's one movie house, where he lavished his attentions on the daily changing roster of pictures—usually American B movies interspersed with local productions and serials. "MGM movies were the most unreal, so they were my favorites," he recalled. "The more they were unlike my small town, the better I liked them." Puig especially liked the lavish Hollywood musicals, extravaganzas of elegant costumes, song, and dance, which starred Fred Astaire and Ginger Rogers. He much preferred these over the Argentine productions, which had too much reality for the sensitive youth.

The author went to school in Buenos Aires during the early forties, where he was exposed to "B films to Z films from everywhere." German musicals shared the screen with French dramas, and glamorous refugees from all over Europe poured into the cosmopolitan capital. At the close of the war, the Italian neorealist movement introduced Puig to the work of Rossellini and De Sica, and he was inspired to direct himself, angering his parents, who had hoped for their son to follow a more traditional craft. To appease them, he studied philosophy and language, but in 1956, upon receiving a directing scholarship from Cinecitta, Rome's vast cinema complex, Puig gladly abandoned his homeland. He found friends there, such as the Cuban-born cinematographer Nestor Almendros, but was distressed by the anti-Hollywood, superpolitical bias of the Italian directors, who dismissed a film's storytelling ability as unimportant. "A film had to live only by its soul, its social meaning," he explained. "It was terribly castrating. The arts, I thought, should never be submitted to political custody."

After a year in Rome, Puig moved to Paris. He was much happier in a country whose film critics absolutely revered Hollywood. Puig began to write his own scripts, but found that the films of his childhood kept leaking into his story lines. Eventually he followed the advice of friends, wrote about his own culture, and generated a script that became his first novel, *Betrayed By Rita Hayworth.* From then on, film references knew their place in his work, as universally recognizable counterpoints to the novelist's own characters.

Described as an "independent Socialist," Manuel Puig had to leave Argentina in the mid seventies, in part as a direct result of writing *Kiss of the Spider Woman.* Although the book was about conflict and compassion between two human beings with different value systems, these men were prisoners, and Puig did not shy away from imagining the brutalities they faced inside the Argentine penal system. He explained, "The book is very much about the Argentina of 1973. There was ideological repression and social repression. [Puig does not disguise his own homosexuality.] I wanted to put these two things together. . . . There were moments when people threatened me to leave the country, saying, 'If you stay, you'll be killed.'" After stints in Mexico and New York, Puig moved to Rio de Janeiro, Brazil, in 1982, where his apartment contains shelves of film books and over seven hundred movies on videotape.

When Hector Babenco first read *Kiss of the Spider Woman,* he said he was "invaded" by the novel. The young Argentine-born director knew that it was meant to be translated into film, and didn't rest until he convinced Manuel Puig, who had been disappointed by filmed adaptations of several other books, that he could initiate an accurate transference of the novel's richly detailed character relationship.

Babenco told one journalist, "What attracted me to the novel was the magical way it showed how men of totally different social, political, and psychological backgrounds could become friends and how their friendship could affect their lives. . . .

"My movie aims to destroy the myths of what makes a man a man. What makes a man a man is respect for himself and the capacity to give something to another person. In modern times, the concept of friendship is constantly lost. I wanted to make a picture about people who have nothing to give each other but themselves." It seems logical to conclude that Babenco's humanitarian approach to the film—as an expression of deep emotions rather than exclusively as a politcal indictment—led Puig to believe that *Spider Woman* would be realized on screen as he intended.

Hector Babenco, the son of poor Russian and Polish Jewish immigrants, grew up in the summer resort of Mar del Plata. He, like Puig, was not comfortable with his childhood environment, and spent his days at the movies or reading at home—a fish out of water in a prosperous community. He admitted, "There was a time I thought I was going to go crazy because my relationship to the outside world was nonexistent." Babenco closeted himself for hours with the works of philosophers and visionaries, sometimes having imaginary conversations with them.

When he was eighteen, Babenco read the time-honored works of wanderlust by the beat gurus, Allen Ginsberg and Jack Kerouac. He took a job as a salesman to raise money, then boarded a ship to travel around the world. Over the next six years, he lived a hand-to-mouth existence in Spain—where he married and had a child—Italy, Portugal, Holland, North Africa, and Puerto Rico. The closest Babenco ever got to film work was as an extra in spaghetti westerns.

His directing career began in earnest when Babenco, fascinated by Brazil's culture, settled in São Paulo. It took him four years to raise a quarter million dollars and shoot his first film in 1975, *King of the Night.* This film set the precedent for Babenco's work, using as its focal point a character, inspired by a real person, who lived on the edge of society, "marginalized," as the director labeled him. "All those people who have no right to participate on an equal footing with other people in the party of life."

Babenco's next film, *Lucio Flavio,* released in 1978, was

about a professional thief who split his profits with the police, who in turn helped shift suspicion away from him. In order to get the movie released at all, Babenco had to include a disclaimer that said the police in the film had false names and that the guilty cops were punished—a blatant lie. The film was an enormous hit at the box office, but Babenco's house was machine-gunned and threats were made against his life.

His 1981 release *Pixote,* which depicted the plight of Brazil's abandoned children, thousands of whom live on the streets, established Babenco as a name director outside South America. For this heartrending film, the director used children from the slums and worked with them, training them to act. The movie came under the scrutiny of American critics and won unqualified raves. "[Babenco] redefines realism in the most unsettling, corrosive terms," declared one writer. "Hector Babenco certainly proved with *Pixote* that he can be gutsy," William Hurt commented admiringly.

Although *Pixote* brought Hector Babenco to much wider attention than he had ever known, that did not guarantee smooth sailing for his next project, the elusive *Spider Woman.* Interestingly, the director first became aware of his fellow countryman's novel thanks to an American, Burt Lancaster. The two met in 1981 when Babenco received a Los Angeles critics' award for *Pixote* and Lancaster sent him a copy of the book. Two weeks later their paths crossed again, at a New York party following a similar critics award for the film. The veteran actor and the intense young director decided to pursue making *Spider Woman,* with Lancaster as Molina, and spent months trying to raise money. Instead, they accumulated rejections. Finally, Lancaster himself decided to take on some production responsibilities, only to suffer a heart attack before he could get to Brazil. There was no way he could continue with the project.

Puerto Rican–born actor Raul Julia was the director's first and only choice for Molina's firebrand cellmate, Valentin. Babenco came up with the idea of William Hurt as the effeminate, romantic, but ultimately courageous Molina after reading an interview with him in *Rolling Stone* in which, among other things, Hurt revealed that the perfect death was being sucked into a turbine. "He's a very tough guy," the director admitted. "He's a little bit paranoiac for my taste, but he's the son of this society that creates crazy people. . . . He's got another approach to life. He doesn't want to be part of the game. He's on his own. . . . In a certain way, I feel he's made of the same stuff as me. . . . Being an actor means for him, in my comprehension, a step in his own life; making a movie is not an end for me but a medium to learn more about myself."

With a major box office attraction like William Hurt in a starring role, everyone connected with the film assumed that financing *Spider Woman* would no longer be problematic. That, however, was not the case. It took over a year before filming actually began in São Paulo, in October, 1983. The actors accepted small salaries and deferred payments—a small sacrifice in return for being part of such a quality product. Eventually, after the director had spent far too much time "living on rumors," the necessary money was obtained, primarily from Brazilian sources with a small percentage from two American investors.

Babenco, who is uncompromising concerning the integrity of his films, wasn't concerned about any undue influence from the U.S.A. In fact, he had already turned down two big studio offers that would have been worth a lot of money, specifically because they would have meant his loss of control. "I'm not American and I'm the boss here," he told a visitor to the São Paulo film set with complete confidence.

Spider Woman had to pass over one last hurdle before it could be successfully realized on screen. Puig had taken great license with the novelistic form, structuring the book completely in dialogue, and jumping abruptly between the characters' conversations and Molina's finely detailed renderings of long-ago film story lines. What Puig could describe in minute detail in written form lost all its nuances and delicacy as a flat film image. Consequently, the film went through five rewrites—two by Babenco and Jorge Duran, and three by the American scriptwriter, Leonard Schrader, before everyone was satisfied.

Schrader was an appropriate choice as screenwriter, since he had an in-depth knowledge of the major Latin American authors, including Manuel Puig. He understood the film's intrinsic political components, having previously authored the political work *Blue Collar*, but saw that his primary artistic challenge lay in writing male characters who were openly emotional, so different from the tight-lipped American screen heroes who were the norm.

"Hector pushed me to write more . . . sentimental than I ever have before," he revealed. "I am more comfortable with American male stoicism as exemplified by stars like McQueen, Wayne, and Eastwood. But there is a total absence of that in Latin American culture. By trying to meet Hector's demands, I achieved much more emotional density to my work than I am used to and he, in turn, complimented me by saying it was much more real than he was used to."

The screenplay, even after five drafts, was subject to further refinement once shooting began, as Babenco, Puig, and Schrader toiled at adapting each stage of Molina and Valentin's growing interdependence from the book to the screen. Hurt, who had opened the book because he thought the screenplay was so excellent, wound up by creating a dilemma for himself. "Their innate structures are indigenous and they should not be fucked with," he acknowledged. "People should not equate one art form with another any more than they should equate a daisy with a rose.

"I was tripping this up. I was going to supplant this indigenous structure of the film with another structure, so I put the book down immediately."

However, this did not relieve Hurt of the more immediate challenge he was facing. He could will himself not to cloud the issue by picking up Puig's novel; there was little he could do whenever he was presented with another unexpected script adjustment. Because of the sheer amount of concentration Hurt required during his rehearsal period before he shot a film—time to grow into an understanding of his character and its relationship to the other players—he was stricken at the prospect of having to alter his character without sufficient time to adjust to the changes.

"I hate script revisions," he vehemently declared. "I prepare every work carefully and I need time to do it. A new word can change the whole scene for me; its delicate structure can be unalterably adjusted. As a process, I find it a little bit too spontaneous.

"This script is being revised all the time, which makes me feel vulnerable. I'm often not sure where I stand and I go into each scene a little unprepared. It's scary, because you're trying to prepare yourself long enough to be surprised in the scene. I don't need any more surprises. Raul's eyes are surprise enough for me any day of the year. That's what I need and to forget everything else—forget all my preparation and relax and allow myself to cover all the distances between the thought and the heartbeat. Maybe they become the same thing. But acting is about listening and too many surprises prevent you from listening to the other actor."

No wonder Hector Babenco's relationship with Hurt proved stormier than the one he developed with Julia, who tended to be a more flexible personality. With Hurt's typically passionate response to the roles he plays, he stretched his interpretation of Molina to the limit, only to be forced by circumstances to contract it somewhat. That situation led to another Hurt maneuver that caught his director by surprise.

At first, he tried playing Molina as an angry man, ready to fling his homosexuality in the face of the world. "But it scared the shit out of everybody," Hurt admitted. It also left no room for contrast with the politically enraged Valentin, who was expected to make righteous outbursts. Babenco voted him down, and Hurt set about playing Molina in a more restrained manner. It gave him a lot of problems. One day, while the movie was still in the developmental stage, Babenco had to go to a meeting, and Hurt made a striking proposal to Raul Julia.

"I said, 'Okay, let's just switch roles.' It's tricky; you have to trust the other person, because when he plays your role he's gonna be telling you how you should play it, and you don't like being told what to do. So I told Raul we could pull the plug on this any time either one of us felt threatened. Well, we just flew." Hurt was inspired by Julia's flamboyant, loving interpretation of Molina, and he proceeded to make Valentin "one tough son of a bitch."

Elated, Hurt sought out his director and urged him to allow his two principals to switch roles permanently. Fortunately, Hurt later realized, Babenco had enough of a grip on the situation to say no. However, the actors had gained so much knowledge about each other's characters that subsequent rehearsals were most encouraging. "We got closer," Raul Julia recalled. "It's a great exercise; it takes courage to do that exercise because your ego can say . . . 'Oh my!' You don't want to see somebody else playing your role."

An abiding friendship was born out of *Spider Woman* between Julia and Hurt. Julia credits the difficult times they shared on the set with the strength of their warm feelings and mutual respect. He said, "In order to have a real relationship with someone you have to go through a process; you can't have it without going through a process in which everything comes up. Not just, 'Okay, let's be friends and that's it, no problems.' It doesn't work like that. You can have acquaintances like that but not relationships.

"We went through everything—as the characters and as the actors; as the people. It was very profound, very human . . . that kind of film [where] you have to go through everything and explore everything."

Kiss of the Spider Woman spends most of its two hours with Molina and Valentin in the cramped cell they share. Molina, the window dresser, is two years into an eight-year sentence for molesting a young boy. The crimes against Valentin are much more serious, as he has acted in direct opposition to the current regime. Molina shows few signs of ill-treatment, but Valentin suffers frequent beatings for refusing to reveal information about his comrades on the outside.

Molina, a flagrant homosexual, makes no attempt to hide what he is or apologize for himself. His method of surviving incarceration is to escape from it, sometimes by relishing the bags of food treats his ailing mother is allowed to deliver, but most often by retelling story lines of movies he has once seen. An avid fan of old films, Molina never runs out of plots to relate, recreating them in loving detail. He tells them, one scene at a time, to the gruff Valentin, who at first has no room in his fevered mind for a drag queen's rhapsodies. Yet as weeks pass and Valentin's secret sorrows multiply, he becomes entranced by the stories, despite himself. Certainly, Valentin is quick to anger, as when he suddenly realizes that Molina is replaying a Nazi propaganda film and seems unaffected by its sickening political orientation. But Molina only cares about the story—he identifies with the heroine who is seduced by the young, strong German officer—and indulges himself in the fantasy.

The reality of their situation is, of course, very different. Molina is forced to make a choice of conscience that would better suit his firebrand cellmate. And Valentin comes to understand first the unselfish love that one person can share with another, and finally, the need Molina has for fantasy. Ultimately, each prisoner must take on an intrinsic part of the other, and this liberates them from their chains.

Kiss of the Spider Woman fused politics and idealism to a story of a romance, in a manner that was understandable to whoever saw it. However, many viewers were taken aback at seeing William Hurt, an acknowledged sex symbol, a confirmed heterosexual who had a two-year-old son with his girlfriend, depicting himself in such a shocking manner. Conveniently forgetting that he had played a homosexual onstage in *Fifth of July*, several of Hurt's advisors told him that acting the role of such an openly gay character might kill his career. He, of course, paid them no mind. Never having seen himself as a macho man notching up bedroom conquests or settling arguments with his fists, Hurt brought authentic empathy to the role of Molina and refused to worry about how it might affect his prospects. (Ironically, the film came out shortly after Hurt had appeared in the misogynistic role of Eddie in *Hurlyburly*, a part that brought him far more hate mail than anything else he has done.)

"I don't want Molina up on a pedestal for a minority group," Hurt maintained. "That's okay with me if it's useful and constructive. But that's not why I played it.

"I feel that the line between the feminine and masculine parts of ourselves moves around all the time," he theorized. "It's not hard for me to identify with a woman. If it were a conscious choice, I would have affectation for this character, but I don't perceive this to be the only way to achieve this purpose.

"His identity of himself is a true thing and has nothing to do with the presumption of others, even though he has to play to them because otherwise they'll kill him. What does a homosexual or a revolutionary do in a society which is bent on their destruction? You hate their hate, but you can't afford that. So often, your ploy would be to turn their appreciation of you as trash by acting trashy—and thereby showing them the worst thing about themselves.

"Here are two characters who start from opposite poles and end up loving each other, and through their love for each other they find greater self-respect. You take these outcasts—and they are outcasts to each other, too, because of the standards they've chosen to bear—and you find that in the destruction of their mistrust they discover that there's a much greater prison and much greater freedom, because they're humane. These two people, even if they don't know it, are looking for the liberation of their own identity. . . . Each ends up pursuing his destiny with more commitment than they had before, because they broke their prejudices."

Babenco, too, wanted his audiences to understand that Molina was not fundamentally different from themselves, whatever their sexual preference. "I didn't want him to play somebody extravagant and flamboyant. I saw him as human, sensitive and just a little affected. In the daytime, he's simply a prisoner. At night, when it's time to tell stories, he wears his robe, lights candles and creates a fantastic, mysterious atmosphere." It was with small gestures that Hurt brought Molina to life. He practiced tidying up the cell and brewing tea. Molina became a character who paid a great deal of attention to the little pleasures of life: his routines of cleanliness brought him relief, the preparation of food and tending of Valentin made him feel purposeful. This was a character who made everyone from the straight world reassess their stereotyped image of a "faggot."

Nine years after Manuel Puig published his novel, *Kiss of the Spider Woman* premiered at the 1985 Cannes Film Festival. As an indication of wonderful things to come, William Hurt was voted Best Actor by the international panel of judges assembled in that southern-France outpost of Tinsel Town.

Janet Maslin, film critic of *The New York Times,* indicated the overwhelming judgment of U.S. reviewers that *Spider Woman* was a major screen accomplishment and instant classic: "From its droll, playful opening to its transcendant coda, it has the mark of greatness from beginning to end." Unstinting in her assessment of its director and co-stars, she heralded the movie as "a brilliant achievement for all of them, staged with the perfect control and fierce originality that make it one of the best films in a long time."

Those critics willing to accept its somewhat unconventional structure, not to mention the possibility of men with polar opposite personalities finding a common ground of compassion and tenderness, believed the film's premise and hailed it. *Time* magazine's reviewer was somewhat suspicious of the stereotypes when exposed to them early on, but went on to say, "The second half of the movie catches you by surprise, not so much by the twists in the plot as by the depth of its emotional impact. Babenco is a passionate filmmaker, and he charges his film with dread and tenderness. The rough spots don't matter; the fate of these two men, and the love that develops between them, is all-important."

Of course, not everyone was comfortable with *Spider Woman,* and criticisms covered a gamut, from displeasure with the film's actual structure—the interspersing of Molina and Valentin's exchanges with imagined fantasy sequences as Molina tells his stories—to discomfort with the revolutionary's acceptance of the homosexual as a person worthy of his love. Mike Clark, writing in *USA Today*, pronounced the film "more an intellectual than a dramatic experience, and that's disconcerting." *New York* magazine's David Denby was amongst the movie's harshest judges, sensing "an element of homosexual wish fulfillment," and apparently, not liking that idea very much. He also labeled the recreated film sequences, which featured Brazilian actress Sonia Braga, "inept moviemaking," and chastised Leonard Schrader for dialogue he judged "canned." "If we're going to have movies in which one character represents imagination and the other action," wrote Denby, "then by all means let the language flow in torrents. But Schrader's dialogue lacks verve and rhetorical flair—it's resolutely downbeat, and we're left squirming in discomfort as the all-too-sensitive gay communion reaches its inevitable conclusion. . . . This paean to the powers of imagination has its starchily humanitarian side; the movie finally sinks from the weight of its own nobility." Apparently, even in the outwardly sophisticated milieu of well-traveled film reviewers, certain prejudices die hard.

The good reviews obviously did outweigh the bad, because, even without the power of a big-money studio behind it, *Kiss of the Spider Woman* was a smash, recouping many times its costs. Raul Julia's performance as Valentin brought that underrated actor a decent measure of recognition, but it was William Hurt who, transforming himself into the compelling feminine Molina, was judged brilliant. "Hurt's mesmerizing performance is no stunt," said *Time.* "Risking foolishness, he achieves a heartbreaking metamorphosis." The actor who was not in this business for big dollars or celebrity hysteria was suddenly being talked about as a serious contender for an Academy Award.

Considering Hurt's track record of dealing with the demands of Hollywood, no one would really have been that surprised if he decided to give the Oscar presentations a miss. Certainly, his behavior at one of *Spider Woman*'s opening night parties in New York was true to Hurt's unpredictable style. At least one journalist attempted to engage him in conversation, only to receive a rambling stream of philosophy and invective, topped off with the command, "Don't treat me like God!" Mortified, she made no further attempt to get anything coherent out of him on that occasion. The actor often lived up to his characterization as "Hurt the Curt," though he later acknowledged, in a different interview, that much of his defensiveness stemmed from fear and insecurity.

Ultimately, after being told by Steven Spielberg that he was refusing a major honor by not going, Hurt did in fact attend the Academy Awards ceremonies in March, 1986. He believed, he said, that actors should not be forced to compete against one another, especially by some outside judgment-callers. However, he acknowledged, "If people are going to honor you, how dare you not accept that?"

It seemed unlikely that William Hurt would actually win the Oscar as Best Actor for his role as Molina. Several obstacles loomed between him and the golden statuette. First of all, Jack Nicholson, an outrageous actor who somehow always managed to stay a few inches ahead of the permissible Hollywood boundaries, was nominated for his role in *Prizzi's Honor,* which had been nominated in several categories. Secondly, *Kiss of the Spider Woman* was not made in America, nor made by Americans. To the film establishment, based in California, this was practically instant grounds for disqualification. Rarely if ever had a star of a foreign production, albeit an American star, been able to achieve this crowning recognition at home. Finally, Hurt was being nominated for his role as an overtly homosexual character, and this in itself was enough to set certain inhabitants of the film community quaking in their boots. Despite its aura of glamour and worldliness, when it came to matters of sexual identity, Hollywood was just another small town, its closeted denizens making sure to stay that way at all costs, so as not to risk their careers. And here was an attractive actor, avowedly heterosexual but secure enough to convincingly play a drag queen. Hurt's part forced the film world's shadowed community to see itself in the mirror, which might have made some of them very nervous.

Yet when the winner of the Best Actor award was announced, William Hurt had indeed run away with the prize. He was on his best behavior that night, making his acceptance speech to the academy and to the millions of fans who watched him on television. "I share this with Raul," he declared, crediting his co-star with sincere warmth. "I didn't expect to be here. . . . I'm proud to be an actor. Thank you very much." If Hurt, as he seemed to be, was stunned, he swiftly recovered with style and grace. This was a triumph for him, and he recognized it. Without compromising one iota of his demanding ideals, working outside the system, and in a challenging, satisfying part, William Hurt had received the highest accolade of his peers.

9

A Lesser God . . .

AND A GREATER LOVE

When William Hurt showed up at the Academy Award ceremonies in Los Angeles in March, 1986, he was accompanied by a petite, dark-haired woman who had already become an intrinsic part of his life. People outside the actor's immediate circle of friends and colleagues wondered about this new lady. She was not a part of the established theatrical community, and the film which would make her a great deal more recognizable, *Children of a Lesser God,* was still six months from being released. However, for almost a year—practically from the first moment they met—William Hurt and Marlee Matlin had been inseparable; their roles as on-screen lovers were echoed in real life by a full-time romance.

Ever since he began working as a professional actor, Hurt had always taken great pains to separate the parts he was playing on the stage or in film from the person he was when the curtain descended. He mistrusted the motives that caused an actor to overidentify with his role, and continually issued reassurances stating that he knew where to draw the line between a manufactured, short-term identity and the real human being.

"I think the characters are true images, because they are as real as the person wants to make them," he conceded, then went on, "but I'm not responsible. I didn't kill anybody. I'm not a lawyer or a janitor. I don't happen to be gay. Doesn't make any difference what I am. That's the best part about the work—if you can just leave it at that and the symbols that are created are good enough to serve. . . .

"I don't see any problem in respecting somebody for either their work or their vision, but I can't accept the misplacement of hero and character. A person can be a hero because of how he does his work and his vision, but these are different things."

Hurt obviously holds to a strong ethic when it comes to the way he is perceived, and until he acted in *Children of a Lesser God* with Marlee Matlin, he was able to keep the individual apart from the vision. However, in this film, two previously disparate paths crossed, and Hurt, rather than fight it, became a much more joyously complete individual because of it. He portrayed James Leeds, a teacher of the deaf who, in falling in love with a deaf student named Sarah Norman, learns about the true commitment of unselfish love. And just as this film gave Hurt's character vivid instruction in how to love unselfishly, so, too, did he fall in love with a deaf woman and realize that he wanted to give of himself in order to understand her world.

It was an unexpected leap into passion for the actor, who had sustained his relationship with Sandra Jennings for several years and still doted on his son, Alex, whom he hailed as his "heart for the future." And Hurt had never been the kind of person to exploit his enviable situation by casually tumbling into bed with the beauties who would have gladly bestowed their charms upon him. His personal commitments were as infrequent and all-encompassing as the parts he opted to play. A new romance was not something this individual would ever take lightly.

But falling in love is never an act of such rationality that it can be selected for time, place, or convenience. And though by becoming involved with Matlin, an almost totally deaf woman just twenty years old when they met (to his thirty-five), Hurt had to set new parameters in his working life, not to mention the need to learn his way into her silent world, it has obviously been worth it to them both.

Following the intensely unpleasant character he had portrayed in *Hurlyburly*—the last project Hurt had completed before *Lesser God*—the actor was more than ready for a role that showed some care and concern for other human beings. On every level—physical and emotional—playing the part of James Leeds was exactly what Hurt needed to take on. This was a character who shared his own obsession with making discoveries about life and truth but had a special difference. Unlike most of Hurt's previous parts, Leeds was the kind of man who expressed himself with grand, sweeping gestures. Nothing was constrained or inner-directed, whether joy, sorrow, anger, shame, or outright bliss. It was a role that brought Hurt face to face with his emotions—all while his hands were being kept busy communicating with the deaf on their terms, in sign language.

"It's about talking and listening," Marlee Matlin explained to a *Newsday* interviewer, communicating through a sign-language interpreter, although she can speak. "It's about deaf people and it's about love and it's about communication. It's about rejection, about giving and taking, about patience." Adapting what had originally been created as a stage work to the screen, with a cast that included a majority of deaf actors, may have also required patience, but the result was successful communication and a moving experience for everyone who was a part of it.

The inspiration for *Children of a Lesser God* dates back to 1977, when playwright Mark Medoff became acquainted with Phyllis Frelich, a deaf actress who had previously been associated with the National Theater for the Deaf. Frelich, an accomplished performer, had expanded the options open to deaf performers by obtaining roles on several prominent prime time television series. (In one memorable "Barney Miller" episode, which drew much notice, she played a deaf hooker.) Medoff decided to write a play for her and had it ready by the beginning of 1979. He was, at the time, chairman of the drama department at New Mexico State University in Las Cruses, so rehearsals took place there. Phyllis Frelich and her husband arrived at the campus and five months of feverish teamwork ensued as the script was refined and polished.

Upon seeing the final product, Medoff's agent realized that this was a very special piece of work and submitted the play to several groups that he believed would be receptive to it. Its first outside production was by the Center Theatre Group and held at the renowned Mark Taper Forum in Los Angeles for six weeks during the fall of 1979.

No one made a big fuss when the play moved to New York a short while later. But even without benefit of a big publicity splash, *Lesser God*'s excellent word-of-mouth began to sell the tickets, and it eventually became a major Broadway hit, one of the most unusual productions to enjoy such a triumph. *Children of a Lesser God* was so acclaimed that it went on to receive Tony Awards for Best Play of the

1979–80 season; for Best Actress—Phyllis Frelich, the first deaf person ever to star on Broadway; and Best Actor—John Rubenstein, who played the teacher, James Leeds. Director Gordon Davidson, who had also worked on the Los Angeles production, was also nominated for an award. In addition to these accolades, the show was given the Outer Critics Circle and Drama Desk awards for that eventful year.

With the play receiving such overwhelming recognition of its excellence, it quickly prompted interest for a screen adaptation. Ned Tanen, at that time the head of Universal Pictures, acquired the film rights but was unable to come up with the right crew or a workable script. The playwright himself tried writing a screenplay, but that did not work out, creating additional tensions. Nor did Tanen's first choice of director. In 1984, when Ned Tanen became head of motion pictures at Paramount, he managed to get the film rights back from Universal. This time he was completely committed to putting together a workable company. He had, in Randa Haines, found the perfect director for this sensitive yet frank and passionate work.

Despite the considerable gains women have made in achieving many professional goals, their numbers in the visual media—particularly in behind-the-scenes positions of power—remain shamefully low. Hollywood's old-and-young-boy networks seem as entrenched as they have ever been, with possible recent concessions to women as scriptwriters. But, whether in feature films or on prime time television, the number of females to have successfully challenged this male establishment still does not amount to more than a handful. The woman Steven Spielberg or Francis Ford Coppola remains years away from operating with a financially secure support system that can back her efforts.

Just possibly, Randa Haines may be the person who will manage to shatter this stalemate. With *Children of a Lesser God* she proved herself completely in control, and over a situation that might have taxed the abilities of a professional with many more films under his or her belt. Haines managed to extract first-rate work from ten severely hearing-impaired cast members, some of them young people who had never acted before, as well as the six hearing principals in the cast. Throughout the months of filming, interpreters and technical advisers were constantly in view to make sure that Haines maintained accuracy—an added pressure. She responded flawlessly to every challenge, including the inevitable determined "discussions" that always took place whenever William Hurt was the star of a film.

"He's a very complex person, and his way of approaching his work does demand a lot of the people he works with," Haines said by way of explanation. "Sometimes we'd disagree and would have to hassle things through. Bill says up front that his philosophy is to make a director's life difficult. But if you're willing to hang in there, you'll come out on the other end with something you both really respect."

The director certainly did not wade into battle unprepared. Randa Haines had a diverse background in film and television work that helped her understand an actor's needs, as well as a director's responsibilities. Originally, she studied acting in New York with Lee Strasberg, but found herself gravitating to the field of directing after she was hired by the School of Visual Arts to work with its directing students. For over a decade, Haines took on various positions in production and script supervision until, in 1975, she had a memorable stay with the Directing Workshop for Women at the American Film Institute. Haines's student project led to her being hired as a writer for "Family," a critically esteemed television series of the late seventies.

Determined to direct, Haines made her television debut with a PBS historical drama, which resulted in a second public television assignment, both garnering critical praise. "Hill Street Blues," one of the few top television series that has consciously maintained an open-door policy toward women, enlisted Haines as director of four episodes. However, it was a television movie dealing with a long-taboo subject, incest, that brought Randa Haines the attention she deserved and made it possible for her to direct *Children of a Lesser God.*

"Something About Amelia" was the kind of groundbreaking film that had to be put under a microscope before being released to the public. It demanded sensitivity and tact, but also a considerable amount of candor, since it had to convey sincere understanding of a widespread, if deeply concealed, problem. On top of that, as it was being made for television, and parents were being urged to watch it along with their children so as to answer any questions, the film had to tread very carefully in order to be passed by the ABC censors. That Haines succeeded on every level was proven by the Emmy she received for "Something About Amelia" the following year.

Once Randa Haines was named director of *Lesser God,* she set about assembling her cast and crew. Another accomplished woman in the film and television industry, Hesper Anderson—who had authored everything from nationally published fiction to plays to episodic television, television movies, and feature films—was given the task of transferring this complex work to the screen. She opted for fidelity to Mark Medoff's original vision, basing her script on the stage play.

Haines immediately realized she had to find a special actor to play James Leeds, the kind of performer who could master the film's complex physical requirements without sacrificing its emotional fabric. Leeds had a staggering amount of dialogue to learn: he not only spoke his own thoughts, but had to communicate to the audience on behalf of the deaf characters, particularly Sarah Norman. In addition, whoever was chosen to play Leeds had to learn how to sign, a demanding procedure that requires several months before any degree of fluency can be attained. For those reasons, the director believed that an actor with stage experience would be less likely to fold under the strain of carrying ninety percent of the film's spoken words on his shoulders. And even though she was quite aware of William Hurt's tempestuous relationships with many of his previous directors, Haines suspected that he was simply the best person to rise to that awesome challenge. Also, she said delicately, "we decided we needed someone who talked to himself a lot so you get used to him muttering."

Finding the right actress to play the proud, angry, defensive Sarah Norman was a much bigger problem, one that took the producers six months to solve. Calls went out to theater groups for the deaf across the United States, as well as in Canada, Great Britain, and Sweden. Thousands of photos—including one of their future star—were viewed and rejected.

The discovery of their Sarah finally took place when the

casting crew received a videotape of a Chicago production of *Children of a Lesser God.* That company hoped that the filmmakers would select their starring actress for the role of Sarah. Instead, Marlee Matlin, playing a supporting role in the production, caught everyone's attention. "She had a dynamic quality, and just the right kind of looks," the casting director summed up. All it took was one read-through in New York with William Hurt, and a screen test a month later in California, and the part was hers. "Marlee took to the camera like a fish to water," the assistant producer commented. "*Afraid* is not in her vocabulary."

Having lost almost all hearing as the result of illness when she was eighteen months old, Marlee Matlin was nonetheless raised as a normal child. Far from being isolated from hearing people, her suburban-Illinois–based parents enrolled Marlee in public schools, where she was able to make friends with both hearing and deaf children. Matlin's parents and her older brothers learned sign language in order to communicate with her.

Still, the obviously bright Marlee was always a rebellious girl, who became angry and frustrated whenever anyone treated her like she was less than clever. In order to help their daughter express her hidden rage, the Matlins enrolled Marlee in acting classes at the nearby Children's Theater for the Deaf. By the time she was eight, the precocious student was already winning lead roles. But once she got into high school, Marlee put acting aside for several years, deciding that she'd rather have fun on dates than be continually competing for parts. Refusing to accept herself as being ineligible for any type of career or relationship, she studied criminal justice at college and became fluent at reading lips.

Matlin hadn't made up her mind as to which direction she ought to go, when a friend suggested that she audition for the *Lesser God* role in Chicago. That was all it took. Although Marlee had, like the character she portrays, at one point dwelt on the obstacles confronting a deaf person, from now on, she would rather just focus on all of her possibilities. "Marlee has a remarkable clarity," William Hurt said admiringly. "I've been waiting for her for a long time."

Although the story is set on the coast of Maine, the movie was filmed in the unspoiled coastal region of New Brunswick, Canada, the first feature film ever to be shot there. After years of delay and months of intricate preparation and rehearsals, filming took place in the autumn of 1985, when the wild country was at its elemental best. Such an untamed land was a most appropriate metaphor for the engrossing story of an unconventional teacher, his group of expressive students, and the tightly coiled woman who wins his heart.

James Leeds is an idealistic and extremely unpredictable instructor of the deaf, who eagerly awaits meeting his newest class, a group of students at the remote Governor Kittridge School. Although some of Leeds's unorthodox teaching methods—such as inspiring his students to "feel the music" of a rock and roll record and eventually sing the nonsense lyrics—don't sit too comfortably with the school's administrators, his results have been undeniable. Leeds begins to work with his new students with verve and gusto, encouraging the ones who are eager to function in the hearing world, while remaining patient with the youngsters whose deafness has led to frustration and hostility.

When Leeds first encounters the sullen, unresponsive

Sarah Norman mopping floors at the school, his curiosity is aroused. Why should this obviously intelligent, undeniably attractive woman hold herself back by refusing to learn to lip-read, speak, or make any other concessions toward the hearing society? Told that Sarah has always been rebellious and is considered a hopeless case, James is unable to ignore her. And she, though highly suspicious of his motives, is curious despite herself. No matter how badly she treats him, cursing him out with gestures and sign language, he keeps coming back with yet another upbeat approach.

Slowly, Sarah begins to allow Leeds into her life, and he gladly seizes every opportunity to become closer. But even after they finally make love and she moves into his home, Sarah insists on using sign language as her only means of communication. James's success in bringing out even the most reticent of his pupils is undercut by his inability to persuade Sarah to consider relating to him in his—and the world at large's—terms. Not until Leeds forces his lover into a confrontation so severe that he almost loses her forever, does the teacher understand that Sarah and her world have something to teach him; they deserve the same kind of respect that he gives to his own culture. And Sarah must also come to an understanding about the way she wants to lead her life, and the person she wants to share it with. *Children of a Lesser God* is a very specific story that concerns barriers of communication between deaf and hearing persons, yet it is readily transferrable to the problems that any two people have in relinquishing control over their own worlds in order to share a new world born of love and understanding.

"The central metaphor is to learn how to listen," Hurt explained. "People don't listen to one another. The teacher is the guy who's really deaf. He's deaf to the girl, deaf to love. The teacher is the cripple." At times, Hurt's own inexperience with the deaf taught him that lesson quite graphically. He often had to speak and sign at the same time, and could not always make himself clear to the deaf teenagers who played his students. One kid really started acting up while in rehearsal, and Hurt felt at a loss as to how, as Leeds, he might get through to him. He reacted instinctively, by getting into a wrestling match with the boy—and made a breakthrough.

Hurt did not face any such obstacles in establishing rapport with Marlee Matlin. Shortly after they met, he bought her a pint of her favorite ice cream, pink bubble gum from Baskin-Robbins. Soon after that, when Matlin did her screen test in Los Angeles, they became lovers. Despite the fifteen-year difference in their ages, and the fact of Hurt's international fame, the couple have been blissfully happy together. The love Hurt feels for her did not come from working in the movie, he has stated. "I would have felt this affection for her if she were a truck driver."

For her part, Matlin acknowledged that she found her boyfriend's vaster experience inspiring. "Bill knows what he's doing," she told *New York* magazine writer David Blum. "He usually has a hold on what he's saying. I envy him sometimes, but he's a professional artist. I'm a freshman and he's a graduate . . . a teacher." The reporter observed that Matlin seemed consumed with her loving feelings for Hurt. "She reminded me of a sorority girl who'd just been pinned by the captain of the football team—forever dropping him into situations and conversations where he didn't seem to belong," Blum wryly noted.

The couple paid little mind to whatever judgments outsiders chose to make about them. By the time *Lesser God* was released, in October 1986, their relationship had already endured for over a year. The previous November, Marlee had moved into Hurt's Central Park West apartment and enjoyed a peaceful life with Bill and his cat, a yellow female named Otis. Hurt installed various devices to make life easier for his housemate: a white light that flashed whenever the doorbell rang, a warning light for the fire and burglar alarm, and a typewriter telephone machine (TTY), which enables Marlee to converse with friends via written messages transmitted over the phone lines. She planned to become a user of Hurt's IBM computer system, one of his favorite tools, in order to communicate with non-TTY-equipped buddies.

Hurt and Matlin appeared unbothered by the stream of attention focused upon them by a curious public and the press. Never had the actor put himself in the position of having an intimate relationship of which the public was so aware. When you came right down to it, any member of the *Lesser God* audience could see the couple, albeit in their film roles, enjoying a number of hot-blooded love scenes, both clothed and unclad. One member of the production crew even took the liberty of calling the pairing ironic. The unnamed individual commented, "Here is Bill Hurt, a man who loves the sound of his own voice, who can talk about Shakespeare, the beauty of birth, and the current state of art deco furniture, all within the span of five minutes—and he's going out with a woman who's deaf!" Apparently, this person chose not to acknowledge the fact that Hurt could discuss any of those things with Matlin in sign language, and if he needed to hear his own voice, there were a thousand hearing people he might talk to.

Still, the young actress, while protecting her boyfriend's privacy, wasn't unpleasant when his name came up in a conversation. Yes, she told one interviewer with some weariness, a lot of people do ask her to discuss Bill (probably because he's so inaccessible most of the time). But aside from remaining noncommittal about the idea of marriage—neither one is ready for it, nor rules it out completely—both Matlin and Hurt openly acknowledge their depth of feeling and commitment to each other.

Of course, unless someone came up with an appropriate part for a deaf actress, in the forthcoming film, *Walter*, *Lesser God* might have been Marlee Matlin's first and only screen triumph. In the meantime, the actress studied at the National Theater of the Deaf, to which her idol, Phyllis Frelich, belongs, and was a sign-language translator for a poetry reading at the Ninety-second Street Y in New York. Matlin believes she will be able to surmount her physical disadvantages and take on other parts in film and television, maybe even create them herself if nobody else does. "I would like to be an actress for the rest of my life," she declared. But Matlin isn't likely to fall apart if that doesn't come to pass. She told *Glamour* magazine that among the other things she'd enjoy doing would be opening a boutique. "I'll go where life takes me," claimed this free-spirited, determined young woman. "I'm an adventurer. Life has a lot of flavors and I want to sample them all."

Children of a Lesser God came to be regarded as a major landmark on many levels, by the deaf community as well as the nation's film critics. There had been previous movies—

Johnny Belinda, The Miracle Worker, The Heart Is a Lonely Hunter—about the deaf, but none in more than fifteen years, and none at all which featured deaf actors in starring roles. While pointing out that the film was primarily oriented to hearing audiences—not every speech was signed, and some signs were obscured by the camera—one educator at a school for the deaf praised it as a learning experience for the hearing world. "Hearing people still have so many misconceptions—like deaf people can't read or dance or cry or laugh. The movie shows that we have the same worries and feelings, abilities and aspirations as anyone else." Marlee Matlin offered a typically gutsier piece of news: "Deaf people have sex too."

Apparently, many reviewers also felt that *Lesser God* had given them something of lasting value, particularly in the interaction between William Hurt and Marlee Matlin. They did have reservations about how well the play worked as reinterpreted on screen. Vincent Canby, writing in *The New York Times,* complained, "it's all too slick. There's scarcely a single moment in it that seems to be spontaneous. It depends on our preconditioned responses to emotional stimuli not of the first freshness." The *Daily News* reviewer, Kathleen Carroll, felt that it was "slow at times," while Robert Massa, writing in *The Village Voice,* labeled the scene transitions "awkward." However, *Newsday* gave the film three and a half stars, and pronounced it one of the few "really good [adaptations] of a stage play to the screen."

These observers saved their superlatives for the actors, and once they got to talking about the principal players, no one held back. "Hurt proves he's one of the most versatile American actors with this wonderfully animated, good-humored performance . . . Matlin was clearly born to play this role and she is astonishingly adept at conveying Sarah's inner frustrations and longings with her facial expressions and body movements," raved the *News*. "Matlin . . . is never—except for one climactic moment—heard from. But she is full of fiery expressiveness and leaves the opinion that she has been speaking audibly throughout the film," said *Newsday*. Even the otherwise skeptical *Voice* writer acknowledged, "William Hurt . . . manages to slip his genuine charm into the excessively jokey, underwritten role. . . . Marlee Matlin . . . and the other actually deaf or hearing-impaired actors, give the movie some eloquence. Their mysteriously fierce concentration almost makes you believe Sarah's claim that deafness is 'not the opposite of hearing but a silence full of sound.'"

And when it came to analyzing the relationship between William Hurt and Marlee Matlin as actors, there arose an interesting polarity of views. Who was the primary influence at work here? According to the *Times*, Matlin "[benefitted] enormously by having an actor of Mr. Hurt's intelligence and skill to work with." Yet *New York* magazine's reviewer, David Denby (who had been openly critical of Hurt in several of his films) believed that, in *Lesser God*, the student had taken control of the teacher, to a fine conclusion: "[Marlee Matlin] focuses a more persistent, direct, and complex demand on William Hurt than any actress he's worked with so far, and he responds with the most fully felt work he's done in the movies."

The accolades poured in for the engaging newcomer, and Marlee Matlin was touted for an Oscar nomination by such critical heavyweights as *Newsweek*'s Jack Kroll, and Jeffrey

Lyons, television reviewer on *Sneak Previews.* With comments such as these in her favor, Matlin went on to win the 1986 Best Actress Award and seems destined to leave a substantial imprint on the entertainment community, assuming it is perceptive enough to generate new parts that suit her unique talents.

William Hurt recognized that his blossoming relationship with Marlee Matlin needed uninterrupted time in order for the couple to get to know one another without the continual butting-in of the press. Consequently, after *Children of a Lesser God* wrapped, he announced his intention to refuse all work until the following spring. Once April 1986 rolled around, however, the actor started the first of two new films he would work on during that year. He began rehearsals for a film called *Destiny,* to be directed and cowritten by Gregory Nava, who had won much acclaim, if not yet widespread public awareness, for his previous work, *El Norte.* A World War Two–era love story about an American family of Basque descent, *Destiny* featured Hurt and Stockard Channing as brother and sister, and also starred the highly regarded young actor, Timothy Hutton. Alive Films, which had released *Kiss of the Spider Woman,* was a principal in this project, along with Embassy Home Entertainment.

In August, the cast flew to Zagreb, Yugoslavia, where the film would be shot, although its story line is centered in Italy and San Diego. During his time abroad, Hurt was visited on the set by Marlee, which certainly must have been a change from the self-isolation he had opted for in his other movies. By the end of the year, William Hurt had been spotted following sportscaster Marv Albert around the corridors of NBC in New York, in preparation for his next role. He had been cast as a journalist for a film to be directed by James Brooks and set in Washington, D.C. Fans and admirers who might have felt deprived without the always intriguing, perpetually intense, frequently unpredictable actor in his yearly screen offering clearly would not be disappointed in 1987. By the end of the year one, possibly two new William Hurt films would be in release.

From the day he began his life's work as a professional actor of stage and screen, William Hurt has received the kind of compliments that would convince any other performer that he had "made it." To viewers and critics alike, he manages to realize extremely different types of roles with a staggering finesse that appears seamless. Hurt takes great care to prepare intricately for every role he plays, yet the end product often seems effortless, the enviable result of his natural talent.

That Hurt does have a natural talent is undeniable. That it was pushed to the surface by the emotional upheavals of his childhood, and later, by his passion for excellence, is also undeniable. But William Hurt is a rarity in this era of the fast buck, the quick kill, and the cheap sentiment. He insists on knowing his parts so intently and fully that people often make the mistake of confusing him with his characters—simply because he has internalized them so well for that space of time. And he never repeats himself, opting instead to stretch into a role with questions and obstacles new to him, invariably, mastering them.

In the face of this ability, it is really no disadvantage for William Hurt to remain personally elusive, privately imponderable. In fact, that may be to his favor. He does not like to talk about himself, or about the specific mechanisms of the parts he plays, preferring to let the film or play speak for itself. When he does open up, it is frequently to raise questions about the issues and goals that all of us in Western society are expected to fulfill. His questioners may not always comprehend the complete context of Hurt's remarks; indeed, they are sometimes so personalized as to elude outsiders. Still, when the dust settles, he has usually put forward a point that keeps people thinking, and that alone is a rare quality in a movie star.

Despite the praises he generates and the awards he receives, William Hurt does not yet consider himself an artist, postponing that achievement into his forties as a future goal. It would not come as a surprise if, when he reaches that plateau, Hurt postpones it again. Process is what motivates him, and process never ends.

William Hurt is an actor of great accomplishments, and a man who is making his way in the world. He asks questions and seeks answers as both. "I think I am on the verge of making the leap of faith," he once said. "I wouldn't say that I have a specifically defined doctrine but it goes very deep. That doesn't mean I can't start out my day saying the Lord's Prayer and end my day by singing a chant. There is something. There is definitely something there . . . we are here for a reason." The extensions of William Hurt as a modern pilgrim make those reasons evident through this one man's extraordinary life.

INDEX

INDEX